Bloom's
GUIDES

Cormac McCarthy's
All the Pretty Horses

1984
All the Pretty Horses
Beloved
Brave New World
Cry, The Beloved Country
Death of a Salesman
Hamlet
The Handmaid's Tale
The House on Mango Street
I Know Why the Caged Bird Sings
The Scarlet Letter
To Kill a Mockingbird

Bloom's
GUIDES

Cormac McCarthy's
All the Pretty Horses

Edited & with an Introduction
by Harold Bloom

CHELSEA HOUSE
PUBLISHERS
A Haights Cross Communications Company
Philadelphia

First Printing
1 3 5 7 9 8 6 4 2

ISBN: 0-7910-7568-0

Chelsea House Publishers
1974 Sproul Road, Suite 400
Broomall, PA 19008-0914

www.chelseahouse.com

Contributing editor: Amy Sickels
Cover design by Takeshi Takahashi
Layout by EJB Publishing Services

Contents

Introduction

HAROLD BLOOM

If there is a pragmatic tradition of the American Sublime, then Cormac McCarthy's fictions are its culmination. *Moby-Dick* and Faulkner's major, early novels are McCarthy's prime precursors. Melville's Ahab fuses together Shakespeare's tragic protagonists—Hamlet, Lear, Macbeth—and crosses them with a quest both Promethean and American. Even as Montaigne's Plato became Emerson's, so Melville's Shakespeare becomes Cormac McCarthy's. Though critics will go on associating McCarthy with Faulkner, who certainly affected McCarthy's style in *Suttree* (1979), the visionary of *Blood Meridian* (1985) and *The Border Trilogy* (1992, 1994, 1998) has much less in common with Faulkner, and shares more profoundly in Melville's debt to Shakespeare.

Melville, by giving us Ahab and Ishmael, took care to distance the reader from Ahab, if not from his quest. McCarthy's protagonists tend to be apostles of the will-to-identity, except for the Iago-like Judge Holden of *Blood Meridian*, who is the Will Incarnate. John Grady Cole, who survives in *All the Pretty Horses* only to be destroyed in *Cities of the Plain*, is replaced in *The Crossing* by Billy Parham, who is capable of learning what the heroic Grady Cole evades, the knowledge that Jehovah (Yahweh) holds in his very name: "Where that is I am not." God will be present where and when he chooses to be present, and absent more often than present.

The aesthetic achievement of *All the Pretty Horses* surpasses that of *Cities of the Plain*, if only because McCarthy is too deeply invested in John Grady Cole to let the young man (really still a boy) die with the proper distancing of authorial concern. No one will compose a rival to *Blood Meridian*, not even McCarthy, but *All the Pretty Horses* and *The Crossing* are of the eminence of *Suttree*. If I had to choose a narrative by McCarthy that could stand on its own in relation to *Blood Meridian*, it probably would be *All the Pretty Horses*. John Grady

Cole quests for freedom, and discovers what neither Suttree nor Billy Parham needs to discover, which is that freedom in an American context is another name for solitude. The self's freedom, for Cormac McCarthy, has no social aspect whatsoever.

I speak of McCarthy as visionary novelist, and not necessarily as a citizen of El Paso, Texas. Emerson identified freedom with power, only available at the crossing, in the shooting of a gulf, a darting to an aim. Since we care for Hamlet, even though he cares for none, we have to assume that Shakespeare also had a considerable investment in Hamlet. The richest aspect of *All the Pretty Horses* is that we learn to care strongly about the development of John Grady Cole, and perhaps we can surmise that Cormac McCarthy is also moved by this most sympathetic of his protagonists.

All the Pretty Horses was published seven years after *Blood Meridian*, and is set almost a full century later in history. John Grady Cole is about the same age as McCarthy would have been in 1948. There is no more an identification between McCarthy and the young Cole, who evidently will not live to see twenty, than there is between Shakespeare and Prince Hamlet. And yet the reverberation of an heroic poignance is clearly heard throughout *All the Pretty Horses*. It may be that McCarthy's hard-won authorial detachment toward the Kid in *Blood Meridian* had cost the novelist too much, in the emotional register. Whether my surmise is accurate or not, the reader shares with McCarthy an affectionate stance toward the heroic youth at the center of *All the Pretty Horses*.

Biographical Sketch

Charles Joseph McCarthy, Jr. was born in Providence, Rhode Island on July 20, 1933 to Charles Joseph and Gladys McGrail McCarthy. The third of six children and the eldest son, he later changed his name to Cormac, a Gaelic name which means "Son of Charles." McCarthy was raised as a Roman Catholic and attended a Catholic High School in Knoxville, Tennessee, where his father served as a lawyer for the Tennessee Valley Authority. From 1951 to 1952, he attended the University of Tennessee as a Liberal Arts major. In 1953 McCarthy joined the Air Force, where he hosted his own radio show while stationed in Alaska for two years. McCarthy returned to the University of Tennessee in 1957, where he published his first two short stories in the student literary magazine, *The Phoenix*. McCarthy won the Ingram-Merrill award for creative writing in 1959 and 1960 as a result of his publications in *The Phoenix*. In 1961, he married a fellow student, Lee Holleman, with whom he had a son, Cullen. McCarthy left the University of Tennessee without a degree and moved his young family to Chicago, where he worked on his first novel, *The Orchard Keeper*, which was published in 1965. The McCarthys returned to Tennessee where their marriage ended; after the divorce, McCarthy left for Ireland on a traveling fellowship he had received from the American Academy of Arts and Letters. While on the trip, he met English singer/dancer Anne DeLisle, whom he married in 1966 in England.

McCarthy received a Rockefeller Foundation Grant in 1966, and he and Anne settled on the island of Ibiza in Europe while McCarthy completed his second novel, *Outer Dark*. In 1967, the McCarthys moved back to Tennessee, and *Outer Dark* was published to favorable reviews the following year. McCarthy won the Guggenheim fellowship in 1969, and worked on *Child of God*, which was published in 1973. McCarthy and his wife Anne separated in 1976 and divorced later; he then relocated to El Paso, Texas where he currently resides. McCarthy's screenplay *The Gardener's Son* premiered on PBS in 1977, and two years later he published his fourth novel *Suttree* to mixed reviews.

McCarthy won the MacArthur Fellowship in 1981 and used the money to support himself while working on his fifth novel, a western based on historical events in Texas and Mexico during the 1840s. Published in 1985, *Blood Meridian, or The Evening Redness in the West*, is considered by many to be McCarthy's finest novel, marking a turning point in his career.

In 1992, Cormac McCarthy published the first volume of *The Border Trilogy—All the Pretty Horses—*which became a *New York Times* Bestseller and a National Book Award recipient. *All the Pretty Horses* brought McCarthy notoriety and a wider readership than he had ever experienced. In 1994 McCarthy published his play *The Stonemason*, as well as the second volume of *The Border Trilogy—The Crossing*. The final volume of *The Border Trilogy—Cities of the Plain—*was published in 1998. In 2000 Miramax adapted *All the Pretty Horses* into a major motion picture starring Matt Damon and Penélope Cruz.

The Story Behind the Story

Before the publication of *All The Pretty Horses*, Cormac McCarthy had been writing and publishing his work for thirty years. His five prior novels never sold more than 5,000 copies a piece. *All The Pretty Horses* sold over one hundred thousand copies within the first six months of its publication, already more copies than all of his previous books combined. Critics and devoted readers considered the popular success long overdue. If McCarthy himself was surprised by the novel's extreme popularity, he didn't publicly admit it. Although the accomplishment of *All The Pretty Horses* brought McCarthy's books out of obscurity, it did not lure him into the spotlight—he gave no public readings or book tours.

Despite the lack of commercial success before *All The Pretty Horses*, McCarthy garnered a faithful cult of readers and favorable critical response to his work. Reviewers often compared McCarthy's work to that of William Faulkner, admiring his dense, lyrical prose and profound, provocative themes. His characters are often wandering outcasts, his narratives resonating with apocalyptic visions. McCarthy's narratives mix beauty with stark violence, creating complicated and unforgiving worlds. "There's no such thing as life without bloodshed," McCarthy has said. (Woodward, 30) Because of his small following, McCarthy was tagged a "writer's writer"—a brilliant author whose work is read only by other writers.

His first four novels—*The Orchard Keeper* (1965), *Outer Dark* (1968), *Child of God* (1973), and *Suttree* (1979)—are set in the Appalachian South, and most readers and critics marked McCarthy as a Southern writer. However, McCarthy then complicated this categorization with the publication of *Blood Meridian, or the Evening Redness in the West* (1985), the first of several novels, including *All The Pretty Horses*, that are set in the West.

Except for a short time in Europe, McCarthy spent much of his early writing years (1967–76) living in Tennessee. However, three years before the publication of *Suttree*, the last of his

Southern novels, he moved to El Paso, Texas. He conducted extensive research for his next book, the first of his Westerns, by traveling to all of the locales that appear in the book and learning Spanish. *Blood Meridian*, by far the most violent and disturbing of all of his novels, takes place in the 1840's in Texas and Mexico. It is an apocalyptic novel focusing on an unromanticized and revisionist history of how the West was won— through extensive destruction and bloodshed. With the publication of *Blood Meridian*, Cormac McCarthy proved himself to be a writer who could not be easily categorized. This novel opened a window into the West, and *All The Pretty Horses* appeared ten years later as the first installment of the Border Trilogy.

Considered more accessible than his other work, *All The Pretty Horses* (1992) joins a coming-of-age narrative, a love story, and linear, action-driven plot, a combination that won McCarthy popular appeal. Recognizing the popularity of the narrative, McCarthy commented in the only interview he has granted to date: "There isn't a place in the world you can go where they don't know about cowboys and Indians and the myth of the West." (Woodward, 30) Although *All The Pretty Horses* manifests many qualities of a conventional western, the novel also complicates the traditional genre and questions the prevailing cowboy myth.

The reception of McCarthy changed dramatically with the publication of *All the Pretty Horses*. McCarthy had already won critical respect throughout his career. For example, in 1981, he was awarded a MacArthur Fellowship, also known as the "genius" grant. Yet his work did not garner a wide readership or extensive scholarship until *All The Pretty Horses*. The novel became an immediate bestseller. *All The Pretty Horses* received the National Book Award and the National Book Critics Circle Award for fiction in its first year of publication. Following this success, Vintage International reprinted all of his previous books in paperback. *All The Pretty Horses* was also made into a Hollywood film directed by Billy Bob Thornton (2000). Scholarly attention continues to grow steadily, and the Cormac McCarthy Society, devoted to the studies of his work, formed in 1993. The first Cormac McCarthy Homepage <www.cormacmccarthy.com> formed in 1995, and hosts the Society, as well as provides a bibliography for McCarthy scholarship and a forum for discussion of his work. In addition, the book's runaway success earned the remarkable first printing of 200,000 copies for McCarthy's next two novels, *The Crossing* (1994) and *Cities of The Plain* (1998). *The Crossing*, the second book of the Border Trilogy, surprised many readers by not continuing with the saga of John Grady Cole, the protagonist of *Horses*. Instead the novel chronicles the young boy Billy Parham's attempt to return a she-wolf to the wild. However, with *Cities of The Plain*, the last installment of the trilogy, McCarthy unites the two protagonists of *All The Pretty Horses* and *The Crossing*.

Despite all of this success, Cormac McCarthy continues to live quietly, guarding his solitude and privacy. Disliking self-promotion and publicity, he has only ever permitted one interview, at the urging of his agent and publisher. He does not go on book tours, teach classes, or take part in writing conferences, and he does not write book reviews or blurbs for other writers' books. For most of his career, McCarthy didn't have an agent; the first time he was published he sent his manuscript to Random House, unsolicited, where it was acquired by Albert Erskine, who had been the long-time editor of Faulkner. Erskine remained as McCarthy's editor until he retired, and when *Horses* was published, McCarthy moved to publisher Alfred A. Knopf. Cormac McCarthy lives such a quiet, hidden life that novelist Madison Smartt Bell has stated that McCarthy has "shunned publicity so effectively he wasn't even famous for it." (Bell, 9) Although McCarthy continues to remain removed from the public eye, his work is no longer unknown. *All The Pretty Horses* immensely expanded McCarthy's readership, which had eluded him for so many years, and prompted important critical responses to his work.

Works Cited

Bell, Madison Smartt. "The Man Who Understood Horses." *New York Times Book Review* 97 (May 17, 1992), sec. 7:9.

Woodward, Richard B. "Cormac McCarthy's Venomous Fiction." *New York Times Magazine* (April 19, 1992): 30.

List of Characters

John Grady Cole is the sixteen-year-old protagonist of the novel. With his grandfather's death and the certain loss of the Grady ranch, the dispossessed cowboy rides to Mexico with his best friend Lacey Rawlins. Along the way they pick up the impulsive "gunsel," Jimmy Blevins, who leads them into danger. Grady's respectable skills with horses secure work for him at La Purísma ranch where he falls in love with the owner's daughter. This affair and the incident with Blevins lead to trouble with the Mexican authorities. Stoic, brave, and idealistic, John Grady embarks on an adventurous, difficult journey into adulthood. After enduring the chaotic and often violent experiences on his journey, John Grady eventually reaches a deeper understanding of people and the natural world.

Lacey Rawlins is John Grady's best friend who accompanies him to Mexico, La Purisma ranch, and the Saltilla prison. Seventeen-year-old Rawlins is more realistic and sentimental than John Grady. Although he questions Grady's decisions, such as the choice to help Jimmy Blevins, Rawlins is a loyal friend. Rawlins' exasperation with Blevins and his worries about foreboding troubles distinguishes him from Grady. Moreover, his candid emotions play off Grady's stoicism.

Jimmy Blevins is a young runaway who follows John Grady and Rawlins to Mexico. Most likely a horse thief, he is also a sharp shooter. Rash and stubborn, Blevins's impulsive actions propel the plot. Even after his death, Blevins continues to be a strong presence, affecting John Grady's consciousness.

Alejandra Rocha is the beautiful daughter of Don Héctor Rocha, owner of La Purísma ranch. She and Grady begin a love affair, stopped short when Grady is arrested. Alejandra, also a lover of horses, carries a sadness inside of her that John Grady cannot comprehend until much later in the novel.

Dueña Alfonsa is Alejandra's great-aunt and godmother. A wise, yet stubborn woman, she forbids John Grady to become involved with Alejandra. She functions as a storyteller, explaining the history of the Mexican Revolution and her own personal plight to John Grady, while at the same time revealing her powerful role in the present events. Although Grady's "enemy," the Dueña Alfonsa also tries to teach him about truth.

Don Héctor Rocha y Villareal, owner of La Purísma ranch, is a wealthy horse breeder. He favors John Grady, and promotes him to be his assistant. Rocha trusts John Grady until he finds out that he has been involved with Alejandra, and then he dispossesses him from the ranch.

Emilio Pérez is a man who may or may not be imprisoned in Saltillo, but who clearly runs the prison's workings. He meets with Grady to warn him that he can only buy his way out of prison. This character acts as another "teacher," lecturing Grady on reality.

Captain is the police captain of Encantada, where Grady, Rawlins, and Blevins are accused of horse-thievery and murder. The captain executes Blevins. Later, Grady avenges his friend's death by reclaiming the horses and taking the captain hostage.

John Grady's father, now divorced, lives in a hotel in town. A surviving prisoner of World War II, his father is dying of cancer. Grady rides horses with his father and seems close to him, yet his father does not fight for him to run the ranch. He encourages Grady to reconcile with his mother.

John Grady's Mother is an actress who spends much of her time away from the ranch. She refuses to give the ranch to Grady, stating that he is too young, and instead sells the ranch to the oil companies. She has no interest in ranches or horses, and wants to live a more exciting life. Although John Grady goes to see her on the stage, he does not reconcile with her.

Although **John Grady's grandfather** never appears alive in the novel, his death begins the story. The grandfather is described as a tough, stubborn cowboy, the family member John Grady most admires and hopes to resemble.

Summary and Analysis

All The Pretty Horses opens with the death of John Grady Cole's grandfather, and in a larger respect, with the demise of the rancher's way of life. The novel starts in mid-September 1948 at the Grady ranch in western Texas, where the plains and ranches are slowly giving way to oil companies, highways, and industry. The novel's first setting, near San Angelo, is located about 125 miles from the Mexican border.

The beginning of *All The Pretty Horses* establishes particular themes and symbols that appear throughout the novel and also initiates the novel's central plot—the physical and metaphoric odyssey of sixteen-year-old John Grady Cole. Early images depict themes of alienation and loss. For example, when John views his dead grandfather at the ranch, he hears a train "boring out of the east like some ribald satellite of the coming sun howling and bellowing in the distance" and feels it moving beneath his feet. The duality of the Texas landscape—the pastoral and the industrial—depicts how the retreating rural landscape cannot withstand the force of the pervasive industrial West. John Grady Cole fully grasps the meaning of this loss. As his sense of loneliness and estrangement increases in the scenes leading up to his journey south, John Grady Cole is "like a man come to the end of something." He cannot stave off the influence of industry over the land, just as he cannot change his mother's decision to sell the ranch to the oil companies.

The traditional narrative of the pastoral ranch, and the heroic, rugged life of the cowboy begins to topple immediately. Critic Sara Spurgeon posits that McCarthy introduces familiar icons such as the western cowboy, then strips away the layers to reveal its emptiness, as first demonstrated in the loss of the ranch. She describes the life of Grady on the ranch as "a mask, a rose-colored and stereotyped cliché of the national symbolic barely hiding the falseness at its core," a myth which McCarthy dismantles in the early pages of the novel. (Spurgeon, 27) Similarly, in his essay "Cowboy Codes in Cormac McCarthy's Border Trilogy," Phillip A. Snyder examines the issue of the shifting cowboy identity and its displacement in the modern world, "the ambiguous space between the myth and the reality of the modern West." (Snyder, 200) The sale of the ranch displaces John Grady Cole, and also symbolizes in a larger context the displacement of the modern-day cowboy in America. Yet the predominant *myth* of the cowboy lives on, and this myth encourages John Grady Cole to venture southward. In order to find a way of life that resembles his grandfather's, he will journey to a different frontier, one that he believes will offer the codes and heritage of the Old West.

Before leaving for Mexico he approaches his parents and their divorce lawyer about the ranch, hoping to assume his grandfather's role and continue family tradition. Although his parents have been separated for much of his life, the divorce is only recent—another event that contributes to John Grady Cole's estrangement. His mother, the sole inheritor, dismisses John Grady's idea of running the ranch himself, and his father, haunted by his POW experiences during WWII and now dying of cancer, has no energy or interest in lobbying for his son. He explains that he returned from the war changed: "I ain't the same as I was. I'd like to think I am. But I ain't." His son refuses to believe this: "You are inside. Inside you are." Regardless of what his father might say, John Grady prefers to maintain his own idealized, heroic image of his father. Like his role-model grandfather who would "never give up" believing his son-in-law was alive when he was missing in action, John Grady is headstrong in his beliefs.

As the only son in the Grady family, John believes he is entitled to ownership of the ranch. According to critic Dianne Luce, the protagonist starts out confusing "the ardor of his desire with his right to attain its object." (Luce, 156) He believes he has a right to entitlement and ownership, and when he realizes he will not be handed over the ranch "he sets out to regain this lost paradise in another country." (156) Family tradition and ownership, then, has been broken in the grandfather's death, as symbolized in the vanishing of the family name: "The Grady name was buried with that old man the day the northern blew the lawnchairs over the dead cemetery grass.

The boy's name was Cole. John Grady Cole." Although he cannot control the family land, he does have the link to his grandfather's name; for the duration of the novel, his name appears as John Grady, emphasizing his strong connection to his grandfather.

John Grady, both physically and metaphysically dispossessed from the family land, finds neither satisfying answers in this changing environment nor compelling reasons to stay behind. His ties to his divorced parents are tenuous. His father, the more understanding of the two, grows weaker day by day, and becomes less of a presence in his son's life. John Grady sometimes stands outside his father's hotel at night to "look up at the room on the fourth floor where his father's shape or father's shadow would pass behind the gauzy window curtains and then turn and pass back again like a sheetiron bear in a shooting-gallery only slower, thinner, more agonized." Although his father encourages John Grady to reconcile with his mother, the mother and son remain estranged. His actress mother spends little time at home—she has dreams of the stage, not of horses. When John Grady hitches a ride to San Antonio to see her perform in a play, he feels confirmed that he is not a part of her life. He watches the play and does not find answers, about their relationship or about the world: "He'd the notion that there would be something in the story itself to tell him about the way the world was or was becoming but there was not. There was nothing in it at all." Apparently, his mother does not know he was in the audience; silently, he watches her walk out of a hotel on the arm of another man.

In the first chapter, the women in John Grady's life make brief, yet significant appearances. Not only does Grady feel estranged from his mother, but he also feels this way about his girlfriend, Mary Catherine, who has "quit" him for an older boy with a car. When she suggests they continue to be friends, John Grady replies, "It's just talk." She counters, "Everything's talk isnt it?" and he answers, "Not everything." This telling line emphasizes John Grady's belief in actions, not words, a doctrine that will work for and against him throughout his journey. In addition to establishing the young Grady's troubles with women, Luce suggests this early scene also portrays the protagonist's youthful immaturity:

> In a confrontation with Mary Catherine before he leaves home, she behaves with openness and poise, offering John Grady a continuing friendship, while he sulks and attempts to shame her. Their contrasting levels of maturity suggest that Mary Catherine may display good judgement in preferring an older boyfriend, car or no car.
>
> (Luce, 158)

Although heroic and often fearless, John Grady is still a boy, with a somewhat selfish view of the world. Yet, he also seems to at least faintly grasp the importance of relationships. When his friend Rawlins dismisses Mary Catherine, "She ain't worth it. None of em are," John Grady doesn't buy into this cliché, arguing, "Yes they are." The significance of this statement resonates later—when Grady will risk his life for the woman he loves.

For now, John Grady feels more comfortable around horses than women. He likes to ride his horse Redbo along the old Comanche road, which leads to Mexico, foreshadowing his own journey south. On this ride he envisions the Comanches, "nation and ghost of nation passing in a soft chorale across the mineral waste to darkness bearing lost to all history and all remembrance like a grail the sum of their secular and transitory and violent lives." The Comanches were eradicated and pushed out from their land, and their banishment evokes John Grady's own departure. His father makes a direct comparison: "We're like the Comanches was two hundred years ago. We dont know what's goin to show up here come daylight. We dont even know what color they'll be." Ironically, neither John Grady nor his father seem to grasp that their own ancestors killed or forced out the Comanches. The cowboy myth of the West silences the history of the Comanches, argues Sara L. Spurgeon, suppressing the horrible violence that nearly eradicated a people: "John Grady, in his innocent acceptance of the noninnocent myth of the sacred cowboy realizes only faintly this debt of blood ..."

(Spurgeon, 27) Yet, as the novel continues, McCarthy will both affirm and undercut John Grady's romantic view of cowboys, masculinity, and the honor code of the Old West.

The plot of *All the Pretty Horses* is more linear than McCarthy's earlier works; however, this more traditional structure should not be equated with simplicity. The novel is a *bildungsroman*, posits Gail Moore Morrison, a coming of age story defined as:

> an archetypal American genre in which a youthful protagonist turns his back on civilization and heads out—into the forest, down river, across the sea, or as in John Grady's case, through desert and mountain on horseback—into the wilderness where innocence experiences the evil of the universe and risks defeat by it.
>
> (Morrison, 178)

The physical journey to Mexico also acts as a metaphoric journey that will provide important experiences for Grady's maturation into adulthood, and awaken him to a deeper understanding of himself and the world. Critic James D. Lilley suggests that the novel is actually more complex than a traditional *bildungsroman* because Grady actually desires to go back into the past, rather than to discover new land: "John Grady does not want to *extricate* himself from the past—establishing a new beginning, divorced of all precedent, on the frontier; rather, his journey down into Mexico becomes an elegy to the Old West, an attempt to move backwards in time to a place where the codes of the Old West are still valorized." (Lilley, 274) This Old West frontier represents Grady's imagined version of the past. Whether going backward or ahead, he journeys to Mexico because there is nothing left for him in San Angelo. His grandfather is dead and his father is dying, and John Grady has been rejected by his mother and his girlfriend. As he succinctly tells Rawlins, "I'm already gone."

The first chapter is the longest of the four, establishing reoccurring themes and imagery, developing the characters, evoking the power of setting, and plotting the journey. The first part is broken down into many sections, analogous to Grady's fragmented world. Nearly six months pass in the first thirty pages, yet the actual journey into Mexico comprises a significant two-thirds of the chapter. Before the ranch is officially turned over to the buyers, John Grady and his best friend, seventeen-year-old Lacey Rawlins, saddle up their horses and ride off in the night "like thieves." They are searching for a better way of life. As they ride through Texas, crossing roads and highways, stopping to undo fences in order to ride across the country, they are hopeful about reaching their dreams of "Paradise," a country where nothing can fence them in.

The beginning leg of the journey is light-hearted and optimistic; humor accompanies the terse, short dialog between Grady and Rawlins. McCarthy uses a mix of short, unpunctuated dialog, which moves at a quick pace, in addition to the more poetic, lyrical passages of exposition. McCarthy also uses Spanish throughout the novel. Grady speaks both Spanish and English, often playing the role of the translator. As a mediator between languages, he moves more freely between borders.

Through his speech and actions, Grady emerges as likeable, adventuresome, and independent. Clearly, he acts as the leader of the two friends (although he later claims they are equals). Grady, prone to stoicism, endures all of Rawlins questions and worries about life and death and religion. Early on in the trip, Rawlins expresses his apprehension, asking Grady if he ever felt ill at ease. Grady's direct, succinct answers portray his self-confidence and his faith in action: "If you're someplace you aint supposed to be I guess you'd be ill at ease. Should be anyways." Significantly, Grady obviously does not feel ill at ease as they head into Mexico, referring once to a map that shows nothing but blankness below the Texas border, whereas Rawlins seems to foresee the danger. Rawlins, the more rational of the two, often expresses his doubts about their actions. However, Grady, as the charismatic, courageous leader, does what he wants to do, and Rawlins always follows his lead.

Before Grady and Rawlins cross into Mexico, they are joined by Jimmy Blevins, a young "gunsel." As dramatic foils, Rawlins and Blevins contribute to the development of John Grady's character. Rawlins, the sensible one, does not trust Blevins. Several times over the course of the journey, he tries to convince Grady to leave Blevins behind. However, John Grady refuses to abandon the boy—he feels protective of him, drawn to his unpredictable, reckless nature. Blevins possesses the same characteristic that attracts Grady to horses: "What he loved in horses was what he loved in men, the blood and the heat of the blood that ran them. All his reverence and all his fondness and all the leanings of his life were for the ardent-hearted and they would always be so and never be otherwise." John Grady often lacks foresight, ignoring Rawlins' rightful prediction: "Something bad is goin to happen." Grady remains sympathetic to Blevins, an unreliable thirteen-year-old runaway. Blevins has already lied to them about his age, his name (Rawlins accuses him of hijacking the name from a radio evangelist), and most likely about the bay he rides, which Rawlins believes was stolen. Like Grady, Blevins also naively identifies with the "old way" of life, referencing the Comanches and insisting on cooking the shot rabbit "the way the Indians did."

Blevins is determined to live by the codes of the Old West at any cost. His stories and tall tales characterize him as a quixotic cowboy, who reasons that the boys should let him travel with them because "I'm an American," a moment the critic Diane Luce suggests is a nod "that he is 'one of us' and that Mexicans are 'other,' and indeed a reflection of John Grady's unacknowledged opportunism." (Luce, 160) Although John Grady does not consciously ride into Mexico to take what he believes belongs to him, he is aware that this land represents "what I'm here for." The cowboy myth can no longer be sustained for John Grady in Texas; however, Mexico presents him with an opportunity to discover this idealized way of living.

The three boys cross the border into Mexico. Naked, they ride their horses through the Rio Grande, the baptismal scene symbolizing rebirth: now they belong to a different frontier, what they perceive as land of opportunity. The moment of their crossing is depicted as momentous and joyous:

They rode up out of the river among the willows and rode singlefile upstream through the shallows onto a long gravel beach where they took off their hats and turned and looked back at the country they'd left. No one spoke. Then suddenly they put their horses to a gallop up the beach and turned and came back, fanning with their hats and laughing and pulling up and patting the horses on the shoulder.

The boys' mood reveals triumph and accomplishment, and at this point they show no reservations about their future in this foreign territory.

The crossing of the Rio Grande is a literal and metaphoric crossing of borders, a reoccurring theme in the novel. Borders represent lines between Mexico/America, wilderness/civilization, past/present, as well as between people of different race, economic class, and ideals. McCarthy blurs these very lines, argues Mark Busby, by creating a "complicated way of knowing the world that is not simply black or white, good or evil, life or death, but is an oxymoronic melding, an ongoing dialectic between the forces of death and life, end and beginning." (Busby, 10) This scene of crossing the Rio Grande represents not only the crossing over of physical borders (between Mexico and America), but also the very beginning of John Grady's maturation (from boyhood to manhood).

The crossing into Mexico also propels the novel's plot. Arriving in the Mexican state of Coahuila, the Americans camp for the night, and in the morning ride again. They pass through the small town of Reforma and buy cups of "cactus juice" from a young Mexican girl. The description of the landscape reveals the poverty in Reforma: "Half a dozen low houses with walls of mud brick slumping into ruin." The boys ride on until they come to a small *estancia*, and the family who lives there invites them in to eat and rest: "They ate by the oillight at a small painted pine table. The mud walls about them were hung with old calendars and magazine pictures." Critic John Wegner comments that the narrative "explicitly mentions the existing poverty in its descriptions of the houses and/or appearance of the natives," to portray the difference in economic classes and to underscore the truth in Dueña Alfonsa's history, as told later in the book, about the failed revolution. (Wegner, 106) In addition to revealing the poverty of the local people, the supper scene with the destitute family depicts a moment of kindness among strangers, and serves as a contrast to some of the more dangerous interactions which lie ahead. The still light-hearted tone of the novel hints at changing when Blevins falls off his chair and quickly leaves the table. For the duration of the night, he stays outside of the house because he doesn't "like to be laughed at." Blevins hates to be humiliated—for anything to challenge his masculinity and toughness.

The next morning when the boys continue on their journey, they pass through dry scrublands and into mountains. The setting itself almost becomes another character in the novel, shifting from scene to scene, always alive and in constant motion. When Rawlins asks, "Where do you reckon that paradise is at?" he refers to their hope for a promised land filled with ranches and horses. Unlike their homes in Texas, oil pumps and fences do not overrun this land. The boys believe, however naively, that they have found untouched country, a paradise overflowing with opportunity: "Big Rock Candy Mountains... [with] lakes and runnin water and grass to the stirrups." Although the landscape often shifts from the beautiful to the harsh, a place barren and "blood red," a land that will not protect or save them, the setting is always imperative to the plot, themes, and characters. As critic Alan Cheuse explains, in McCarthy's hands the setting becomes more than merely background. Landscape resembles "a force to reckon with rather than a mere reflection of mood." (Cheuse, 140) He posits that character motivation and setting are intertwined, with the setting providing insight into the characters' interior thoughts. For example, when John Grady "lay a long time listening to the others breathing in their sleep while he contemplated the wildness about him, the wildness within," character and setting reflect each other.

The light-hearted, optimistic tone darkens more noticeably as the journey pushes on, with the lightening storm providing a clear transition into the trouble Rawlins has correctly forecasted. The storm, a catalyst for the plot and a major shift in the buoyant tone, depicts Blevins' irrational, wild behavior. Fearful of being struck by lightening, he strips off his clothes and takes shelter under a dead cottonwood. When he comes out of hiding the next morning, he has lost his horse, his pistol, and all of his clothes, save his underwear and cowboy hat. His nakedness exposes his youth and vulnerability, further emphasized when they ride into a wax camp and a man offers to buy Blevins. The wilderness continues to become more threatening. Morrison maps out the structure of their journey, and the symbolism of the shift in landscape:

> The landscape becomes progressively wilder and more barren: roads, trucks, and stores give way to desert and mountain. The animals that they hear or fear become progressively more ferocious: coyote, wolf, lion. The food that they eat becomes increasingly more primitive ... the people they encounter become increasingly savage.
>
> (Morrison, 183)

After the lightening storm, the Mexican setting slowly transforms into something darker and more violent. Instead of seeing birds in flight, the boys witness a flock of birds caught and impaled on cholla thorns: "Gray nameless birds espaliered in attitudes of stillborn flight or hanging loosely in their feathers. Some of them were still alive and they twisted on their spines as the horses passed and raised their heads and cried out but the horsemen rode on." This gruesome image creates an unsettling mood and foreshadows violence to come.

In the pueblo of Encantada, where they spot Blevins' horse, Rawlins again tries to convince Grady they should abandon Blevins: "This is our last chance. Right now. This is the time and there wont be another time and I guarantee it." Rawlins, already irritated by Blevins who makes him feel "uneasy," has grown more fearful and apprehensive of this strange country. Although Grady understands Rawlins' logic, "he knew that he was right in all he'd said," he refuses to give up ideals of heroes and cowboys for a safer way of life. Grady also values loyalty, and his sense of loyalty grows stronger over the course of the journey—loyalty to family, friends, and, as revealed later, loyalty to his lover. In her provocative essay "Boys Will Be Boys," Nell Sullivan points out how the absence or containment of women in McCarthy's westerns destabilizes gender roles, that by "divorcing femininity from women and allowing the male performance of both gender roles, McCarthy in effect creates a closed circuit for male desire." (Sullivan, 229) The loyalty between Rawlins and Grady, "I wouldn't leave you and you wouldn't leave me," emphasizes their close camaraderie. Rawlins does not want Blevins to join their friendship, but Grady will not leave the boy: "You realize the fix he's in?" Grady agrees to help Blevins, and Rawlins follows Grady's lead, but Blevins' single-mindedness and rash behavior puts all of their lives at risk. He takes his horse and wakes the townspeople; men on horses chase after the boys. Riding his bay out of town, with pistol shots and howling dogs trailing behind, "all out bedlam," Blevins is the epitome of the lawless cowboy. He takes the road alone because he knows he can outrun the mob, and sends Grady and Rawlins into the country. The land, open and exposed to the elements, offers no shelter. The two boys constantly look over their shoulders, worried about lions and dubious shepherds. Their optimism has disappeared in the heart of the wilderness, as they stay alive by hunting animals and camping in the fields.

However, before anything terrible befalls them, the boys spot a group of *vaqueros*, Mexican cowboys, and in this moment they feel a sense of safety and rejuvenation. The landscape itself reflects their mood shift:

> The grasslands lay in a deep violet haze and to the west thin flights of waterflow were moving north before the sunset in the deep red galleries under the cloudbanks like schoolfish in a burning sea and on the foreland plain they saw vaqueros driving cattle before them through a gauze of golden dust.

This moment, with its "golden dust" portrays a moment of hope and optimism. The boys join the men, helping them drive cattle to a ranch. Alejandra makes her first brief appearance, with John Grady watching her, "still looking down the road where she'd gone." Whereas the chapter opened with loss—the grandfather's death—it ends on a note of hope and optimism. Hired at the ranch, Grady and Rawlins join the community of cowboys, thereby sustaining their dream of living the western ideal.

At the end of Chapter one, during the boys first night at the *hacienda*, McCarthy establishes the dream-like mood at La Purísima. Rawlins, hopeful that they have discovered the old Western way of life, asks Grady, "This is how it was with the old waddies, ain't it?" Grady tells Rawlins several times to go to sleep. Rawlins asks Grady how long he'd like to stay here, and he answers, "About a hundred years. Go to sleep." Critic Edwin. T. Arnold examines the role of dreams and visions in the novel, stating, "Chapter 2 might very easily be read as an extended dream experienced in that sleep." (Arnold, 151) The line stating that Grady would like to stay a hundred years also alludes to the fantasy of the place—their time at the *hacienda* resembles a fairytale. Here the boys have found what they were looking for, and they hope to hold onto this forever—or at least for a hundred years.

Like the landscape of mountains and barren plains in the first chapter, the setting in **Chapter two** interweaves with character and plot. The *Hacienda de Nuestra Señora de la Purísima Concepción* contains beautiful country with cattle, wild horses, and wide open spaces. The ranch stretches 27,500 acres, with mountains to the west, and the southern and eastern parts settled on the basin floor, rich with streams and lakes. The description achieves a dreamy, magic effect: "In the lakes and in the streams were species of fish not known elsewhere on earth and birds and lizards and other forms of life as well all long relict here for the desert stretched away on every side." Here the boys have the opportunity to live out their fantasy of cattle-ranching in an Old West paradise.

Unlike the Grady ranch, La Purísima has not been sold—it has remained the family for 170 years. The wealthy owner,

Don Héctor Rocha y Villareal, travels in his own private airplane, owns a thousand head of cattle, and runs an elaborate horse-breeding program. After John Grady demonstrates his impressive skills by breaking sixteen wild horses in four days (with assistance from Rawlins), Don Héctor promotes him as his personal assistant, and Grady moves out of the communal bunk and into a private room in the barn. For most of this chapter, John Grady is separated from the rational Rawlins. This isolation provides him the opportunity to fully embark upon his romantic, individualistic ideals. Chapter two further develops the plot of John Grady's coming of age, providing situations that test his convictions. He acts with both deception and passion, refusing to bow to authority. This chapter also introduces the romantic plot with Alejandra and builds on themes of borders—as between class and race, and myths and reality.

Grady, the heroic cowboy, demonstrates his skill for horse training in the long, detailed horse-breaking scene. He flaunts his love for the creatures, coupled with his desire to master them. He continuously strokes the horses and talks to them, easing their fear and anxiety, but he also vows to control them, considering himself "the voice of the breaker still running in their brains like the voice of some god come to inhabit them." Grady appears to be conflicted in desiring to either become a part of the wild or to master the chaos. Horses, a focal point of the novel, appear in plot, characterization, theme, and landscape. Critic Tom Pilkington asserts that the horses "represent the vital life force of the universe." (Pilkington, 319) Grady breaks and rides horses, dreams of them, and has philosophical conversations about them. For example, when John Grady and Rawlins are catching wild mares for the *hacendado* (Don Héctor), John Grady speaks to the old cook Luis about the nature of horses. Luis explains the horse "shares a common soul and its separate life only forms it out of all horses and makes it mortal ... if a person understood the soul of the horse then he would understand all horses that ever were." The common connection between horses is not parallel to humans because "among men there was no such communion as among horses and the notion that men can be understood at all was probably an illusion." For Grady, horses represent an element of life and nature in its purity. Grady dreams of these "ardent-hearted" creatures: "Horses still wild on the mesa who'd never seen a man afoot and who knew nothing of him or his life yet in whose souls he would come to reside forever." Thus, horses serve to disrupt the border between nature and humans. A continuous theme in McCarthy's work, asserts Sara L. Spurgeon, is that the "world of men and the world of nature are not really separate ... and the task of reconnecting those worlds drives many of his characters." (Spurgeon, 37) Although Grady admits he "ain't a horse," he dreams of fusing the wildness of the horse with his own humanness.

Horses also serve as a connection between John Grady and Don Héctor. Horses represent the common language, overriding any barriers between Spanish and English. John Grady and Don Héctor develop a type of father-son relationship. However, this relationship begins with deception. In their first meeting Grady lies to the father-figure. Don Héctor asks him "Why are you here?" and John Grady simply answers, "I just wanted to see the country, I reckon. Or we did," choosing not to tell his boss about Blevins or the situation in Encantada. As the reader later discovers, Don Héctor already knows about Encantada, and he is offering Grady the chance to tell the truth. Yet John Grady hides the truth; he secures his status on the ranch "through lying and deception that are sanitized in his mind by his conviction of his good intentions." (Luce, 157) This initial lie then hints to another consequential deception— that of his affair with Don Héctor's daughter.

Alejandra, who rides the Arabian horse proper English-style, captures John Grady's attention as soon as he sees her: "He'd half meant to speak but those eyes had altered the world forever in the space of a heartbeat." Alejandra, attracted to John Grady's skill with horses, also loves the creatures. As horses contribute to the relationship between John Grady and Don Héctor, they also help form the relationship between the lovers, specifically noted in the way John Grady's sexual prowess is symbolized by the famous stallion that Don Héctor bought to breed with his wild mares. For example, Grady rides the horse while the animal is still in mid-copulation, "lathered and dripping and half crazed," and "he loved for her to see him riding it." Alejandra, however, is not meek or afraid. As Morrison points out, she "challenges both his authority and his mastery with her own skill as horsewoman" when she dismounts from her Arabian horse and insists on riding the stallion bareback. (Morrison, 181)

John Grady ignores the warnings not to become involved with Alejandra, the most significant of these coming from Dueña Alfonsa, the girl's great-aunt and godmother. She invites John Grady to meet with her, ostensibly to play a game of chess. After John Grady wins the first two games, Alfonsa wins the third by using a move he had never seen before. Missing two fingers from a shooting accident in her youth, the seventy-three-year-old Dueña notices the scar on Grady's cheek, noting, "Scars have the strange power to remind us that our past is real. The events that cause them can never be forgotten, can they?" She wants Grady to understand the power of the past, its living history, and that La Purísima does not symbolize a clean slate for him.

Although she later calls herself his enemy, Alfonsa also saves Grady, and tries to teach him important lessons about truth and fantasy. She warns John Grady that Mexico "is another country," indicating despite the dream of living at the *hacienda*, this place is not his home. Here, rules and customs exist that he does not understand. She explains she wants to protect Alejandra because "here a woman's reputation is all she has." According to critic Linda Townley Woodson, the Dueña Alfonsa represents one of the various mentors John Grady encounters in Mexico who try to "make him understand the truth." (Woodson, 150) However, after this first meeting with Alfonsa, John Grady seems confused, or unwilling to follow her advice. He tells Rawlins he is not sure if he gave Alfonsa his word not to see Alejandra. Rawlins accuses Grady of having eyes set on the daughter and "on the spread." About the land, Grady genuinely tells him, "I aint thought about it." Rawlins doubts him: "Sure you aint." Although Grady only admits to having "eyes for the daughter," Rawlins insinuates that he must be at least subtly aware of what a marriage to Alejandra could mean for him—a chance to live (and possibly own) this Paradise. However, this marriage will not be permitted; Don Héctor, cross-breeder of horses, will not allow a "similar experiment in crossbreeding between his daughter Alejandra and the Texas import." (Morrison, 181) John Grady, fully aware of the danger in becoming involved with Alejandra, listens quietly to Rawlins' prediction: "What I see is you fixin to get us fired and run off the place." Although Grady realizes the truth of this statement, he will not abandon his passion, no matter the consequence. Neither will Alejandra.

When Alejandra arrives at his door five nights later, he lets her in, and their passionate affair begins. Like Grady, Alejandra refuses to follow rules she considers stifling, even wrong. She resents her great-aunt's infringement on her privacy, asserting, "I won't be treated in such a manner." Critics have accused McCarthy of creating female characters who are two-dimensional, undeveloped, and only populate the pages in order to serve an "immediate function in relation to the boys." (Owens, 65) However, other critics have pointed out the complexity of Alejandra and her great-aunt. For instance, as Morrison notes, Alejandra acts with passion and rebellion; "overtly the aggressor" in the relationship, she initiates the love affair. (Morrison, 181) For nine nights she visits Grady. Part of their passion may stem from the secretiveness of the affair. When they ride their horses to the lake their lovemaking is "sweeter for the larceny of time and flesh, sweeter for the betrayal." Although John Grady understands class and nationality prevent the possibility of marriage, he also hopes that his own free will and independence can shake the foundation of the hacienda's rules.

The borders of nationality and class play a part in the condemnation of their affair; however, Sara L. Spurgeon makes a convincing argument that the United States and Mexico are represented not as opposites but as "mirror images of each other," (Spurgeon, 30) and similarly, Alejandra and Grady are more twins than opposites. For instance, Grady's family, who also owned a ranch and employed servants, actually resembles Alejandra's family. Furthermore, Grady and Alejandra are both youthful lovers who "still see the world as they wish it to be, from the privileged position of their social classes, cocooned in the fragile paradise of their respective ranches, where the descendants of the peoples their ancestors conquered are now servants and outcasts." (Spurgeon, 31) Yet now Grady works for Alejandra's father, securing him in a different (lower) status. The borders separating them may overlap, yet in spite of John Grady's hopes, they cannot be completely broken down. Despite the lovers' similarities, John Grady recognizes that something tugs at Alejandra which he cannot yet understand: "he could see her throat move in the light and he saw in her face and in her figure something he'd not seen before and the name of that thing was sorrow."

The critic Gail Moore Morrison observes the allegorical allusions in the novel, detailing John Grady's expulsion from "Paradise," and arguing that the end of his "fall from innocence" leads him through a rite of passage into adulthood. (Morrison, 179) Thus, John Grady, independent, courageous, and rebellious, symbolizes the biblical Adam—for the moment living comfortably in Eden, but on the brink of expulsion. Similarly, critic Tom Pilkington notes the American-ness of the Adam figure, noting Grady "believes in individualism, free will, volition. He thinks every man born on this planet is an Adam, free of memory and external constraint, able to shape his illimitable "self" in any way he chooses." (Pilkington, 320) What Alfonsa wants Grady to understand is that he is not "free of memory," that actions carry responsibility and consequences. Owens also agrees that John Grady represents an "American Adam" figure—self-reliant, heroic, romantic protagonist who faces and rises above challenges. (Owens, 67) If La Purísima symbolizes Eden and John Grady represents Adam, then Don Héctor is God, and for a short time John Grady "lives in a beautiful place, walking with Don Héctor, like Adam with God in the cool of the evening, as they talk about the innermost secrets of horses," and the boy's expulsion occurs when he "chooses Eve over God." (Owens, 83)

Whereas Pilkington examines how philosophical issues of fate and individualism complicate the novel from being a traditional Western, Owens argues that McCarthy reinforces stereotypes and fictitious cowboy myths: "McCarthy pursues a very Anglo-male trail, playing to the common ethos of a cowboy-loving crowed. Without altering basic mythic types or classic plots, he plays with poetic language and thematic motifs." (Owens, 66) Perhaps a space exists between these arguments, the novel both embracing and subverting traditional cowboy themes. For example, the highly sophisticated narrator establishes a distance from the more naïve perspective of John Grady, creating a space between his ideals and the narrative's reality. Commenting on the spaces between borders, Snyder focuses on the cultural myth of the cowboy versus the reality: "This may be the most significant border McCarthy explores in the trilogy—the one that lies in the gap between the ideal and the real..." (Snyder, 201) He views McCarthy as critiquing and renovating the myth, while at the same time "reaffirming the cowboy codes which structure the behavioral patters of John Grady..." (201) For example, some of these behaviors, such as Grady's loyalty, are admirable, useful qualities. The narrative carves out a space, perhaps, between the borders of reality and idealism. The problem lies in Grady's inability to differentiate between the two, his confusion of the myth of the cowboy as giving him a right to entitlement (of the ranch, of Alejandra).

Despite this American Adam's views on free will, he cannot topple this power structure, nor can he topple the ranch's owner. Although he hopes he will be given what he believes he's entitled to, Grady soon loses everything—the narrative actually critiquing instead of endorsing a desire for power. Over a game of pool, Don Héctor advises Grady, "Beware gentle knight. There is no greater monster than reason." He seems to be supporting notions of heroism and action, yet at the same time, he makes his power stance clear, easily beating Grady in the game. Grady understands the weight of Don Héctor's power. When he finds out that Alejandra will leave, he acknowledges, "there was nothing to tell her and there was nothing to do." Three days later, while Grady and Rawlins hunt wild mares in the mountains, Don Héctor's pack of grey-hounds enters their camp. Later the readers learn that Alejandra has told her father about their love affair. Although the vengeful, betrayed father does not kill Grady, he turns him over to the Mexican authorities. Grady and Rawlins return from the mountains, and their brief time in Paradise has ended. The Mexican police lead them away in handcuffs. After three months of living at La Purísima, John Grady has been expelled from Eden, without Eve. Now he must wake up from the dream.

Chapter three spans seven weeks, starting with the boys' arrest and ending with Grady's solo journey back to the ranch. Mirroring the journey John Grady and Rawlins made from Encantada to the ranch at the end of Chapter one, Chapter three begins with a forced departure from La Purísima and a return to Encantada, the pueblo where Jimmy Blevins retrieved his horse. Previous dialog and images have foreshadowed this turn of events: early in the novel the boys are described leaving their homes "like thieves;" when they cross the river they resemble a "party of marauders;" the friends joke about being mistaken as *desperados*, romanticizing the meaning. Ironically, now they are accused of murder and horse stealing. It is not lost on either of them that Alejandra's father arranged this arrest—that essentially they are here because John Grady stepped over boundaries of class, race, and nationality. When Rawlins complains that he had tried to reason with Grady, he characteristically replies, "I know you did. But some things aint reasonable." This chapter serves as a major rite-of-passage in John Grady's coming of age journey, challenging him in grave, consequential situations that will finally begin to alter his idealistic understanding of the world.

After living for three months on a spacious ranch, John Grady and Rawlins are now locked in a small cell without light, joining an old Mexican man who doesn't know how long he's been imprisoned or why, and Jimmy Blevins, whose feet have been broken by the police, and who looks "scrawny and ragged and filthy." After John Grady questions him, Blevins admits that after escaping on his horse, he later returned to the pueblo to retrieve his pistol and then shot two men, killing at least one. Nothing has changed about Blevins; dangerous and reckless, he is also immature and does not seem to grasp the severity of his situation. Instead of taking responsibility for killing a man, he asks, "What choice did I have?" Rawlins had correctly predicted that associating with the "gunsel" would only lead them to trouble. Now his irritation and uneasiness turns to fear: "We're dead men. I knew it'd come to this. From the time I first seen him." Grady does not share this sentiment; he shows no signs of worry or fear—the first night in the cell, he easily dreams of horses, continuing with his notion of freedom and Paradise. His dream combines his desire to be a part of that wildness, where "he was among the horses running and in the dream he himself could run with the horses ... they moved all of them in a resonance that was like a music among them and they were none of them afraid." Freedom is still a part of him, something within his grasp. Furthermore, whereas Rawlins breaks down in fear at the captain's accusations and torture, admitting to the false charges of murder and horse stealing, Grady shows no signs of intimidation. Because John Grady, the stoic, heroic cowboy, refuses to be intimidated, his "manhood" is never questioned or compromised. He will not admit to something that is false: "There aint but one truth," said John Grady. "The truth is what happened. It aint what come out somebody's mouth." Snyder comments on this stoicism as being one of the characteristics of the cowboy code, arguing that although Grady may not be talkative, he is "eloquent both in action and in discourse, particularly when that discourse is tied to behavior." (Snyder, 223) For Grady, truth is not found in words, but in action and experience. Not yet ready to accept consequences, he still does not seem to realize the impact of his lying to Don Héctor.

After three days the prisoners are transported to Saltillo, and on the journey, Jimmy Blevins is taken from the truck and executed. Whereas Rawlins, the voice of reason, often foreshadows events correctly, he does not have the capacity to even imagine this grave situation. Rather, this time it is Grady who correctly predicts the succession of events. The setting for the execution, the hot, dusty desert, where "there was no cloud, no bird," also highlights the horror of a place without sustenance or hope. Thunder and lightening appear in the horizon, unnerving Blevins and foreshadowing his death. The truck then leaves the road, moving further into wilderness, and then stops in a meadow where the remains of ruined, abandoned buildings still stand.

The cinematic narration powerfully captures the mood of the scene and the characters, without analyzing or explaining motives. This flattened, minimalist language, with the high tension depicted in actions, expressions, and setting, renders the scene even more disturbing and shocking. Although McCarthy employs a sophisticated narrator throughout the novel—the prose a combination of Faulkner's lush, expansive style and Hemingway's minimalism and objectivity—this particular scene is told in the minimalist style, or what critic Nancy Kreml calls a transparent style. The transparent style includes descriptions of both mundane acts and more intense, significant scenes—such as Blevins' execution. "By describing any action (even the buying of baloney) and therefore drawing out attention to it," explains Kreml, "McCarthy suggests that it is significant; by leaving it uninterpreted, he allows the reader to supply many contexts for its possible interpretations." (Kremel, 140)

In the execution scene, before the police take him away, Blevins removes his boot to give John Grady his roll of cash. Then he is led away, "mute and terrified," and hobbling with one boot. This image echoes the earlier image of Blevins half-naked in the wax camp, again emphasizing his vulnerability and youth. The captain, with his arm around Blevins, leads him to the grove of ebony trees, while John Grady and Rawlins wait in "the strange land, the strange sky." The minimalist description illuminates the terror: "Rawlins looked at John Grady. His mouth was tight. John Grady watched the small ragged figure vanish limping among the trees with his keepers." Rawlins refuses to believe this could actually be happening, "They caint just walk him out there and shoot him, he said. Hell fire. Just walk him out there and shoot him," and just as he says this, they hear the pistol shots. The sound is "a flat sort of pop," Blevins' death swallowed up by the expansive, unforgiving landscape.

Kreml categorizes McCarthy's other predominate narrative style as opaque—as depicted in the more expansive, complex, poetic passages. (Kremel, 141) For example, the prison at Saltillo is described in opaque language:

> The prison was no more than a small walled village and within it occurred a constant seethe of barter and exchange in everything from radios and blankets down to matches and buttons and shoenails and within this bartering ran a constant struggling for status and position. Underpinning all of it like the fiscal standard in commercial societies lay a bedrock of depravity and violence where in an egalitarian absolute every man was judged by a single standard and that was his readiness to kill.

This prose style uses metaphors, imagery, and judgments, without leaving the scene open for interpretation.

If the ranch symbolizes a cowboy's paradise, then Saltillo represents the opposite, a dark, hellish underworld of violence and corruption. At night the boys sleep "in iron bunks chained to the walls on thin trocheros or mattress pads that were greasy, vile, infested," and during the day, they fight for their lives. Previously, the boys had no trouble conjuring Paradise, with their ideals of cowboys and free land, but the depravity and harsh conditions of prison is completely inconceivable to them. Rawlins admits, "I never knowed there was such a place as this." If Grady was experiencing a dream during Chapter two, sleepwalking during his time on the ranch, here he is fully awakened to reality. (Arnold, 53)

For the first three days the boys undergo attacks and beatings by the other prisoners, with Grady encouraging Rawlins to fight back: "They either got to kill us or let us be. There aint no middle ground." On the fourth day they buy necessities: clothes and soap and soup. When Rawlins complains of what has happened to them, "all over a goddamned horse," Grady counters, "Horse had nothin to do with it," perhaps beginning to acknowledge his own mistakes. During his time at the prison, he receives a fierce education on the workings of the world. The prison strips away ideals; here no myth can protect him.

The chaotic prison operates on an old set of corrupt rules, in which freedom, like anything else, can only be bought. John Grady has been told how they can leave this prison, first by the captain from Encantada who warned him he would be killed if he did not make "arrangements," and then by Emilio Pérez. A mysterious character, Pérez may or may not be a prisoner, but he clearly runs the inner workings of the prison. The meeting with Pérez echoes previous scenes with Don Héctor, the Dueña Alfonsa, and the captain, in portraying Grady as an astute listener. Although Grady may place more faith in actions, not words, he knows how to read between the lines and navigate others' parables and metaphors. He is capable of strategy, as demonstrated in his superb chess-playing abilities.

Pérez, in cloaked words, offers the boys protection and possible freedom for a price. Although Grady understands the offer, he turns down Perez; true to his character, John Grady refuses to succumb. Later, after Grady and Rawlins have refused the offer, another prisoner knifes Rawlins. He is transported to a hospital. As in Chapter two, John Grady is separated from Rawlins, and this physical distance reflects the expanding psychological distance between the friends.

When Grady meets with Pérez a second time, Pérez warns him that the authorities will pick a crime to charge him with if he does not act and make "arrangements." In addition to addressing the significance of the novel's historical content, John Wegner's essay also examines the role of economic class, arguing that "poverty and the powerlessness inherent in poverty transcends nationalities." (Wegner, 107) Grady's Americanism will not save him from the fate of prison. When he refuses Pérez for the second time, Pérez scoffs at Grady's ideals, claiming that Americans associate qualities of good or evil with objects, where as the Mexican does not attribute human qualities to objects: "Americans have this problem always I believe. They talk about tainted money. But money doesnt have this special quality." This scene serves as another example of the teachers Grady encounters, another version of a lesson about truth. When Grady tells Pérez he is not afraid of dying, Perez answers, "That is good. It will help you to die. It will not help you to live." Although Grady may glean parts of Perez's lecture about survival, he does not give into Pérez's corrupt demands. His refusal conveys a mix of his morals and stubbornness, reinforcing his character as being independent and self-sufficient.

Grady's fight for life or death occurs in the prison's cafeteria. The duel with the *cuchillero*, Pérez's hired man, spans several pages, an extremely descriptive scene detailing the fight for one survivor. This fight symbolizes a turning point, bringing Grady to the edge of death and to a new, more mature place in his coming of age journey. He looks into the *cuchillero's* eyes and sees a "whole malign history burning cold and remote and black." He now becomes a part of this history—in all its ugliness and violence. This scene, written in the transparent language, stresses the utter violence, yet also emanates a kind of grace, describing every single movement for the duration of three pages. After John Grady buries the knife in the *cuchillero's* heart, he walks, dazed, out of the cafeteria, "holding his hand to his abdomen." Blood "sloshed in his boots." The repetitive imagery of blood symbolizes not only the violence of death, but also the theme of the continuum between life and death: "Blood dripped between his outstretched hands. The dark bank of the wall rode up. The deep cyanic sky." The violent, bloody scene, however, ends with hope. He is lifted like a child and carried away to safety by Perez's man.

Grady fully awakens from his long sleep. According to Luce, three events, his arrest, the fact that Blevins killed a man, and Blevins' own death, "begin to wake him, to break the enchantment"—and now that he too has participated in killing—will forever alter his understanding of himself and the world. (Luce, 159) He spends several days healing, for the first time, the reader becomes privy to Grady's fears and sorrows:

He half wondered if he were not dead and in his despair he felt well up in him a surge of sorrow like a child beginning to cry but it brought with it such pain that he stopped it cold and began at once his new life and the living of it breath to breath.

This transition, from child to adult, does not occur in a single moment. The culmination of events has led him to this place— raw, painful, and truthful.

The days in healing represent a type of Purgatory, according to Morrison. He has experienced Heaven and Hell, and now Grady has reached an in-between space, a place of transition. Morrison defines the structure of the novel in terms of what each chapter represents:

> (1) the long *andante* movement of the journey south, on horseback, through an increasingly sterile and incomprehensible wasteland, a false purgatory that foreshadows the false redemption that follows; (2) an *allegro* pastoral interlude in an edenic paradise, rife with fertility of landscape and horse and the promise of Eve, the site of temptation for body as well as for spirit; (3) the staccato expulsion into purgatory of the newly fallen naïf whose education in the dissonances of life's injustices, chaos and confusion has only just begun; and, finally (4), the rendering of judgement, the component parts of which include the failed quest to regain paradise, retribution and a reintegrative odyssey home."
>
> (Morrison, 181)

The three days he spends in the room, near death, represent his most strenuous and significant journey. He thinks about his father's war experience and "knew that terrible things had been done to him there and he had always believed that he did not want to know about it but he did want to know." Whereas before he didn't want to consider the horror that changed his father, now Grady has the capacity, and courage, to fully realize his father's pain. Although he tries to think only of horses, to return to his ideal of happiness, "the right thing to think about," he cannot, at this point. Instead he dreams of the dead: "When he woke he knew that men had died in that room." Horses can no longer represent an idealistic, untainted paradise, but represent only what they are—wild creatures. The death of the *cuchillero* parallels the death of Blevins, whom Grady could not save, a sacrificial death of which Grady is now a part. He emerges from the prison with a more realistic, and darker, understanding of the world.

Ironically, Grady and Rawlins are freed from prison in the way that the captain and Perez had explained—by money; Dueña Alfonsa has paid off the prison. Without much of a choice, Grady accepts this help, even though this freedom comes with a price—he will no longer be able to see Alejandra; his love has been exchanged for his freedom.

Grady has witnessed how money, greed, and the desire for power subvert any kind of idyllic dream, yet he retains his courage and stamina to face and endure this world. Rawlins, however, will return home to safety: "All my life I had the feelin that trouble was close at hand. Not that I was about to get into it. Just that it was always there." For him, this trip to Mexico has only reinforced this feeling. Now that he has experienced this looming trouble, he wants to return to his old life. But, it is doubtful if he can ever return to this innocence. Like Grady, Rawlins too has been changed: "His eyes were wet and he looked old and sad." Obviously shaken by Blevins' death, he continues to turn to Grady for answers, asking him his views on death and prayer. Rawlins tries to exonerate John Grady for murdering the *cuchillero*, stating Grady did not have a choice. However, Grady refuses to be excused: "You dont need to try and make it right. It is what it is." His understanding of the world, in both its beauty and violence, is more complex and expansive than that of Rawlins.

Rawlins takes a bus back to Texas, and John Grady stays two more weeks in Saltillo to have the stitches removed from his face and stomach. Like the Dueña explained, his scars will remind him of his past and make him fully aware of his reality. Then he too leaves, hitching his way back to La Purísima. He stands in the truck bed with his hands outstretched: "As if he were some personage bearing news for the countryside. As if he were some newfound evangelical being conveyed down out of the mountains and north across the flat bleak landscape toward Monclova." This highly metaphoric language, or opaque language, describes Grady as a Christ-figure yet the "as if" also distances him from this innocence. Reality has shaped Grady. Although more aware of authority and power, he has not given up hope.

Chapter four spans from early fall 1950, when Grady returns to La Purísima, to March 1951, when the novel ends with him riding across the Pecos River in Iraan, Texas. To return to the ranch, Grady hitches a series of rides until he makes his way into La Vega. When he shares the ride with the group of Mexican farm workers, they study him and guess by his new clothes that he is going to visit his girlfriend. The men are courteous and kind, giving him their bundles to sit on, and this moment of benevolence resonates with him:

> And after and for a long time to come he'd have reason to evoke the recollection of those smiles and to reflect upon the good will which provoked them for it had power to protect and to confer honor and to strengthen resolve and it had power to heal men and to bring them to safety long after all other resources were exhausted.

Although Grady witnesses filth, corruption, and death, the world is not devoid of hope or goodness, as symbolized in these moments of kindness. Mark Busby comments on Grady's "ultimate recognition of the limitation of self" and to accept, and be grateful for, the others' help and friendship. (Busby, 234) As he walks along the dry dusty road toward Cuatro Ciénagas, strangers stop their work and "nod to him and say how good the day was." Later, when he gets another ride, the workers see his weak condition, and they immediately reach out to help him aboard the truck.

When he returns to La Purísima, he rides the stallion one last time, taking the horse over the rolling land, the same places where he used to ride. When he rests, John Grady lay on the grass and "thought what sort of dream might bring him luck." He tries to imagine Alejandra, the way she looked when he saw her for the first time, and then he thinks of Blevins. He remembers that when he was in prison, Grady dreamt of talking with Blevins about what it was like to be dead and Blevins said "it was like nothing at all." The death of thirteen-year-old Blevins' will always haunt Grady, and he wishes this dark memory would vanish: "He thought perhaps if he dreamt of him enough he'd go away forever and be dead among his kind and the grass scissored in the wind at his ear and he fell asleep and dream of nothing at all." Instead of finding "luck" in his dreams, now they are blank. Reality and dreams are becoming more separate for Grady; experiencing death and killing has changed his idyllic dreams. He cannot let go of Blevins' death, not by imagining his lover or herds of wild horses. This death has become a part of him. Grady no longer lives in his dreams; La Purísima is no longer the untainted Paradise—now the apple is "hard and green and bitter."

In his second meeting with the Dueña Alfonsa, she confirms Grady's suspicion that she bought him out of prison in return for Alejandra's promise to never see him again. She also corroborates that Don Héctor turned him over to the authorities, while reminding Grady that he initially lied to Don Héctor, insinuating his own wrongs. Grady, who has never placed much faith in words, now wants a chance to tell his side of the story. However, Alfonsa argues that nothing can be changed: "But what is done cannot be undone." Alfonsa, unlike Grady, is loquacious and articulate. Through her many experiences, she has come to the conclusion that the world is a "puppet show," with many people controlling the strings. Ironically, Alfonsa also has a hand in controlling the puppet strings by protecting Alejandra from seeing Grady.

The Dueña narrates a detailed history of the Mexican Revolution in 1911–13, and reveals her own personal involvement. Grady, and the reader, learn of the martyred Franscico Madero and Alfonsa's relationship with his brother, Gustave. This historically accurate narrative challenges most historical accounts that tend to focus on General Victoriana Huerta, who overthrew Madero, explains John Wegner. Dueña's narrative reaches beyond "revisionist history," in that it "contends that the 'absent' history, what did not happen, has as great an effect on the history that did occur." (Wegner, 103) In other words, Alfonsa shows how the failing of the Revolution has affected the current state of Mexico. This section also reveals the most direct thoughts on idealism, fate, and independence. Alfonsa describes her younger self as idealistic, romantic, and rebellious, similar to the characteristics she sees in her niece.

As a young woman, Alfonsa was inspired and excited by the ideals of the Maderos, and she believed in the cause Revolution—while still living a very privileged life. She says she never forgave her father for sending her away to Europe, distancing her from the revolution, from her ideals and passion. Alfonsa, most critics agree, is a complex, contradictory character. "Alfonsa is both a radical and a reactionary," writes Morrison. (Morrison, 188) She supports Revolutionary ideals, yet also holds onto and wields her aristocratic power. Robert Jarrett compares Alfonsa to Grady: "If Cole's idealism seeks to nullify history in his belief that he can relive the roles of rancher, horseman, stockbreeder, and romantic lover, then Alfonsita's idealism had consisted of her acquiescence in the belief of Francisco and Gustavo Madera that they could sever Mexican politics from its history and culture." (Jarrett, 103) Yet, as Busby points out, it is Alfonsa, "the former idealist, who most fully challenges John Grady's idealism." (Busby, 235) Woodson also believes that Alfonsa is the "most significant purveyor of truths." (Woodson, 152) What threatens to defeat Grady, offers Spurgeon, is not only idealism but "the hollowness and blindness of his faith—or more properly, the hollowness of that myth upon which he has chosen to place his faith." (Spurgeon, 30) Alfonsa attempts to cure him of this blindness—to coach him on the difference between truths and dreams.

Of all the mentors Grady encounters on his journey, Alfonsa seems to be the most important and her lessons have a lasting impact. She advises Grady: "In the end we all come to be cured of our sentiments. Those whom life does not cure death will. The world is quite ruthless in selecting between the dream and the reality, even where we will not. Between the wish and the thing the world lies waiting." She stresses the importance of differentiating between dream and reality, yet also acknowledges the space between.

The Dueña's monologue takes up several pages, a story within the story, and illuminates Alfonsa's ideas of fate and free will, and her mixed views on idealism. She sees Alejandra heading in the same direction as she once did and does not want to see her defeated or hurt. She will not allow Alejandra to see Grady because she will not risk her great-niece's reputation in a patriarchal society, but she also rejects his idealism, perhaps comparing him to the Maderos. For instance, Woodson posits that Alfonsa "judges him to be unsuitable for her niece because of his willingness to use, as does the rest of her world, the language of desire and power." (Woodson, 153) She has witnessed the terrible bloodshed and violence of her country and doesn't "believe knowing can save us. What is constant in history is greed and foolishness and a love of blood and this is a thing that even God—who knows all that can be known—seems powerless to change." Ironically, although she criticizes power, Alfonsa wields the most power in this family. When John defies her, telling her he intends to see Alejandra, who is in Mexico City with her mother, Alfonsa doesn't try to stop him. "She will not break her word to me," the aunt correctly predicts.

Grady leaves La Vega on one of the wild horses that he had broken in those first few glorious days on the ranch, and along his way to Torreón, he meets with a group of children. Here the man of few words tells his story, all that has happened to him since he crossed over the border. Sara L. Spurgeon comments that this parable, "distilled down to its mythic parts" (Spurgeon, 34) shows that while Grady has internalized some of what Alfonsa has taught him, he is reluctant to completely abandon the myth, as he uses stock images to describe Blevins: "This horseman was very young and he rode a wonderful horse." Significantly, the section is not depicted in dialog, but in summary; thus, even in the section where Grady has the chance to speak at length, the readers are still not given the opportunity to hear his voice. His faith in action continues to override speech.

After arriving in Torreón, Grady gets in touch with Alejandra and persuades her to meet him for a night in Zacatecas, to stop over on her way to the *hacienda*. Grady stables his horse, then takes a train to town. When Alejandra arrives, he tells her everything that has happened, narrating his story for the second time, which is again revealed in exposition. When he finishes, she cries, and asks, "How do I know who you are? Do I know the what sort of man you are? What sort my father is ... What are men?" Whereas before Grady didn't trust words, in this chapter he has narrated his story as a way to show the truth:

> I told you things I've never told anybody. I told you all there was to tell.
> What good is it? What good?
> I dont know. I guess I just believe in it.

Grady stubbornly believes he can make things right, but Alejandra, like her great-aunt, understands far too well the implications of history, the power of borders. She is not as idealistic or rebellious as she first seemed—she will not risk losing the love of her father for Grady's love. Alejandra takes John Grady to the site where her grandfather died, a scene which captures her own connection to history, and perhaps aligns her with Alfonsa's view on reality and sentiments. Contrasting with Chapter one, when Grady says good-bye to Mary Catherine, the farewell to Alejandra affects him in a way he has never experienced: "He saw very clearly how all his life led only to this moment and all after led nowhere at all." He never fathomed the sorrow that he once noticed in Alejandra long ago, not until this moment. Unfortunately, love cannot overcome reality; as Alfonsa warned him, he will never see his lover again. After Alejandra returns to her family, Grady, who no longer has a home, gets drunk and becomes involved in a fight. He rides back to Torreón for his horse, and then rides off again. He sleeps in a field, "far from any town" and he listens to the wind and stares at the emptiness around him, and "the agony in his heart was like a stake." The world that once seemed simple to Grady has become complicated.

Grady heads in the direction of Texas, but he stops when he reaches the crossroads, hesitating at the road that leads into Encantada. Then he makes an important decision: "I aint leavin my horse down there." Perhaps he cannot overcome history or change the past, but Grady still believes in the power of the individual to make things right. Despite all of his defeats, he has not lost his courage or his loyalty. Now he will risk his life to save his horse.

The adventurous plot line depicts Grady, the heroic, strong, fearless cowboy, kidnapping the captain, the man who killed Blevins, and saving all of the horses. The scene of capturing the horses involves a shoot-out scene, and an almost impossible plot line—in which Grady manages to escape, although shot in the leg, with his prisoner and all four horses. Although the action may seem unrealistic, McCarthy writes it in such a straightforward way that the reader can believe the story line. This part of the journey, like the opening, represents a more physical, concrete journey for Grady. The structure of Chapter four also mirrors the beginning of Chapter three, when Grady returned to Encantada, by force, on charges of horse-thievery. Now he returns to Encantada by his own free will, to take back the horses that rightfully belong to him. Thus, Grady repeats the same acts in reverse. Like Alfonsa who tries to avenge her own history by controlling Alejandra's destiny, Grady attempts to do the same for himself. Both characters "exact revenge on their past, attaining a paradoxical and problematic freedom within the deterministic patterns of history." (Lilley, 283) The retrieved horses become a retribution for Blevins' death, and the captain, now the prisoner, must worry for his own life.

Grady heads north, completing superhuman acts—driving the horses, pushing on the ill, fearful captain, and pressing a fire-hot pistol into his leg to seal the bullet holes, all while escaping from the men on horseback. Yet the adventure does not only detail the physical feats—the reader also glimpses into Grady's psychological journey. For example, one night Grady dreams of horses for the first time since his imprisonment, and according to Mark Busby, now the dream "is tempered by the disorder, death, and sadness now part of John Grady's knowledge." (Busby, 235) Similarly, critic Edwin T. Arnold notes how instead of running, now the horses move slowly, signifying "a more mature acceptance of the tragic nature of the world." (Arnold, 56) The descriptive language captures the richness of the dream:

> the horses in his dream moved gravely among the tilted stones like horses come upon an antique site where some ordering of the world had failed and if anything had been written on the stones the weather had taken it away again and the horses were wary and moved without great circumspection carrying in their blood as they did the recollection of this and other places where horses once had been and would be again... what he saw in his dream was that the order in the horse's heart was more durable for it was written in a place where no rain could erase it.

Busby explains that the "mixture of sadness and beauty is now part of John Grady's more intricate understanding of the world of responsibility to both humans and animals." (Busby, 236) The horses are no longer the "picturebook" horses in the painting at his grandfather's house. His dreams of horses become more expansive, embodying death and rebirth.

Grady wakes with three armed men standing over him. In this surreal, dreamlike scene, the men give him a blanket, and they take the captain away, probably to kill him. They are described as "Men of the country ... He never saw them again." Grady, now alone except for the horses, rides toward Texas, across a land in which "the wind was cold and he picked his way along the rim country through the sparse swales of grass and broken volcanic rock."

Grady's passage into manhood and his greater understanding of the world is exemplified in the scene where he shoots a doe.

Earlier, in the second chapter, Rawlins killed a buck, and Grady congratulated him, "Hell of a shot." His knowledge of death and participation in killing contradicts this earlier enthusiasm. Now he sits with the doe and "put his hand on her neck and she looked at him and her eyes were warm and wet and there was no fear in them and then she died." He thinks of the captain, Blevins, and Alejandra. In this powerful scene, Grady assumes responsibility for his participation in the killing of another, reflecting on what Alfonsa told him, "At some point we cannot escape naming responsibility." Grady takes on this responsibility, becoming a part of the life and death cycle of all things. Here death and earth and memories blur as one:

> The sky was dark and a cold wind ran through the bajada and in the dying light a cold blue cast had turned the doe's eyes to but one thing more of things she lay among in that darkening landscape. Grass and blood. Blood and stone. He remembered Alejandra and the sadness he'd first seen in the slope of her shoulders which he'd presumed to understand and of which he knew nothing and he felt a loneliness he'd not known since he was a child and he felt wholly alien to the world although he loved it still.

Although he feels "wholly alien" to the world, "he loved it still." This image contradicts a nihilistic vision. Though the world is dark and often uncaring and unforgiving, John Grady continues to embrace this world—for all its ugliness and beauty. He has learned to see both the evil and good, the violence and splendor, and the flux of life and death. Although he may not completely understand this world, he does not turn away from it:

> He thought that in the beauty of the world were hid a secret. He thought the world's heart beat at some terrible cost and that the world's pain and its beauty moved in a relationship of diverging equity and that in this headlong deficit the blood of multitudes might ultimately be exacted for the vision of a single flower.

John Grady's dreams, visions, and actions have carried him to claim responsibility and acknowledge his complicity in death. And the next morning, he awakens knowing his father is dead.

The final chapter's structure parallels the first chapter. John Grady crosses the border, this time back into Texas, again near Langtry. Whereas the first journey was light-hearted and hopeful, his return journey is arduous and lonely. Although he had experienced displacement in the first chapter, with his parents and the death of his grandfather, the emotional impact is much greater in the final chapter. He does not return as an idealistic hero, but as a man who has grown more aware of the complexity of the world. Even the gray, cold land itself seems to be in mourning on this journey, a place where "the air smelled of rosin and wet stone and no birds sang."

He crosses into Texas on Thanksgiving Day, again moving through the river, but this time the mood of the crossing is not exuberant:

> He rode up onto Texas soil pale and shivering and he sat the horse briefly and looked out over the plain to the north where cattle were already beginning to appear slouching slowly out of that pale landscape and bawling softly at the horses and he thought about this father who was dead in that country and he sat the horse naked in the falling rain and wept.

For the first time in the entire duration of his journey, including his grandfather's death, John Grady weeps. Emotionally and physically exhausted, he has completed the most difficult parts of his journey, and even his stoic nature will not suppress his emotions.

For weeks Grady searches for Blevins' horse's rightful owner, and when three different men falsely claim the horse to belong to them, Grady goes to court to tell his story. Again, his narrative of the story is revealed in summary. This time in his telling, the listeners believe him, exonerating him of all crimes. Yet, Grady has not forgiven himself. He goes to see the judge on his own and admits that he killed a boy. Grady believes self-defense is not an excuse: "But that dont make it right." He also admits his guilt in Blevins' death—that he did not try to stop the execution. The day Blevins was killed, Grady was dry-eyed, but now, thinking of both dead boys, his eyes "were wet in the firelight." He admits his true reason for also wanting to kill the captain was "because I stood there and let them walk that boy out in the trees and shoot him and I never said nothin." Grady takes responsibility for his complacency in Blevins' execution, and also for his own deception at the ranch. He says of Don Héctor:

> I worked for that man and I respected him and he never had no complaints about the work I done for him and he was awful good to me. And that man come up on the high range where I was workin and I believe he intended to kill me. And I was the one that brought it about. Nobody but me.

John Grady has changed over the course of his quest, losing his youthful naiveté and selfishness for a deeper respect of others and for the natural world.

Unable to find the rightful owner, with Blevins' horse "a millstone around my neck," Grady travels to Del Rio where the radio minister Jimmy Blevins lives. The minister has never heard of another "plain Jimmy Blevins." After several months, Grady returns to San Angelo, and he reunites Rawlins with his horse, Junior. When Rawlins tries to convince him to stay, to sign up for work on the rigs, Grady says he's going to move on. "This is still good country," Rawlins tries to tell him, and Grady responds, "Yeah. I know it is. But it aint my country." When Rawlins asks him where his country is, Grady admits, "I don't know where it is. I don't know what happens to country." This journey has not provided him with easy answers. He knows he cannot be like Rawlins and return to his life before the journey. Grady has crossed and recrossed and moved between borders, and he continues to be a man in exile.

In the first chapter, Grady attends the funeral of his grandfather, a strange, dismal funeral, where the wind knocked around the chairs and he did not speak with his family. In the last chapter he attends the funeral of his *abuela*, his "grandmother," who raised him and worked for his family for fifty years. At the cemetery he reads the headstones of the dead. This time his farewell, influenced by all that he has experienced and learned, is more emotional. He says goodbye to her and

> then turned and put on his hat and turned his wet face to the wind and for a moment he held out his hands as if to steady himself or as if to bless the ground there or perhaps as if to slow the world that was rushing away and seemed to care nothing for the old or the young or rich or poor or dark or pale or he or she. Nothing for their struggles, nothing for their names. Nothing for the living or the dead.

Grady has been "cured of his sentiments," coming face to face with the meaningless of death, and the delicacy of life. This time when he rides out across the red desert, with the "bloodred dust" and the "red wind," Grady, Redbo, and Blevins' bay are like one long shadow, merged, "paled into the darkening land, the world to come." The borders have been blurred into one. Grady's journey has "taken him into a world of complexity, ambiguity, and ambivalence—a mixture of good and evil, rationality and irrationality, fate and free will." (Busby, 234) In contradiction to the ghost of the Comanches he envisioned in Chapter one, now John Grady passes the living Indians, who watch him pass: "They stood and watched him pass and watched him vanish upon that landscape solely because he was passing. Solely because he would vanish." The Indians know, Luce comments, as now John Grady knows "that romantic dreams of the past or the future have little enough to do with real human experience." (Luce, 163) John Grady is left alone with his horse and the horse of a dead boy to continue into an indifferent world. The ending subverts the classic western structure; John Grady does not win the girl, or the ranch. He has returned empty-handed, save the horses. Although the novel's ending is not optimistic, neither is it entirely fatalistic. Rather, the open ending reflects reality—something complicated, without resolution. Through the course of his journey, the one that continues to beckon him, John Grady has not found easy answers. However, he has learned that he cannot control the workings of the universe, and he grasps the existence of suffering and human limits to this suffering, and he faces all of this with ongoing courage.

Works Cited

Arnold, Edwin T. "'Go to Sleep': Dreams and Visions in the Border Trilogy" *A Cormac McCarthy Companion: The Border Trilogy*, eds. Edwin T. Arnold and Dianne C. Luce. Jackson: University of Mississippi Press, 2001.

Busby, Mark. "Into the Darkening Land, the World to Come: Cormac McCarthy's Border Crossings." *Myth, Legend, Dust: Critical Responses to Cormac McCarthy*, ed. Rick Wallach. New York: Manchester University Press, 2000.

Cheuse, Alan. "A Note on Landscape in All The Pretty Horses." *Southern Quarterly* 30, (Summer 1992).

Jarrett, Robert L. *Cormac McCarthy*. New York: Twayne Publishers, 1997.

Kreml, Nancy. "Stylistic Variation and Cognitive Constraint in All The Pretty Horses." *Sacred Violence: A Reader's Companion to Cormac McCarthy*, eds. Wade Hall and Rick Wallach. El Paso: Texas Western Press, 1995.

Lilley, James D. " 'The Hands of Yet Other Puppets': Figuring Freedom and Reading Repetition in *All The Pretty Horses*." *Myth, Legend, Dust: Critical Responses to Cormac McCarthy*, ed. Rick Wallach. New York: Manchester University Press, 2000.

Luce, Dianne C. "'When You Wake': John Grady Cole's Heroism in All The Pretty Horses" in *Sacred Violence: A Reader's Companion to Cormac McCarthy*, eds. Wade Hall and Rick Wallach. El Paso: Texas Western Press, 1995.

Morrison, Gail Moore. "All The Pretty Horses: John Grady Cole's Expulsion from Paradise." *Perspectives on Cormac McCarthy*, eds. Edwin T. Arnold and Dianne C. Luce. Jackson: University Press of Mississippi, 1999.

Owens, Barcley. *Cormac McCarthy's Western Novels*. The University of Arizona Press, Tucson, 2000.

Pilkington, Tom. "Fate and Free Will on the American Frontier: Cormac McCarthy's Western Fiction." *Western American Literature* 27 (Winter 1993).

Snyder, Phillip A. "Cowboy Codes in Cormac McCarthy's Border Trilogy" *A Cormac McCarthy Companion: The Border Trilogy*, eds. Edwin T. Arnold and Dianne C. Luce. Jackson: UP of Mississippi, 2001.

Spurgeon, Sara L. "'Pledged in Blood': Truth and Redemption in Cormac McCarthy's *All The Pretty Horses*." *Western American Literature* 34, no. 1 (Spring 1999).

Sullivan, Nell. "Boys Will Be Boys And Girls Will Be Gone." *A Cormac McCarthy Companion: The Border Trilogy*, eds. Edwin T. Arnold and Dianne C. Luce. Jackson: University of Mississippi Press, 2001.

Wegner, John. "Whose Story is It? History and Fiction in Cormac McCarthy's *All The Pretty Horses*" *The Southern Quarterly* 36, no. 2. (Winter 1998).

Woodson, Linda Townley. "Deceiving the Will to Truth: The Semiotic Foundation of All The Pretty Horses." *Sacred Violence: A Reader's Companion to Cormac McCarthy*, eds. Wade Hall and Rick Wallach. El Paso: Texas Western Press, 1995.

Critical Views

ALAN CHEUSE ON LANDSCAPE

In his little essay, "Landscape and the Novel in Mexico," Octavio Paz writes of Lawrence, Lowry and the Mexican novelist Juan Rulfo as three artists whose poetic visions "give the landscape its concrete form" rather than vice versa. The landscape in their work, Paz suggests, "does not function as the background or physical setting of the narrative.... It is something that is alive, something that takes a thousand different forms; it is a symbol and something more than a symbol: a voice entering into the dialogue, and in the end the principal character in the story..." (33).

Using Paz's assertions as a standard, a reader can travel through the northern Mexico of *All the Pretty Horses* and notice certain rhetorical patterns that perhaps ought to be regarded as more than mere rhetoric. The landscape, almost a "character" in itself, becomes a force to reckon with rather than a mere reflection of mood. We get a sense of this at the very outset of the novel, while still in the "mapped" portion of the book's geography. West Texas in 1949, when the young protagonist, John Grady Cole, disturbed by disruptive events in his family, rides his horse out from his house to the west, "The wind was much abated," we hear, "and it was very cold and the sun sat blood red and elliptic under the reefs of bloodred cloud before him." John Grady then has a vision of old Kiowa tribes, "nation and ghost of nation passing in a soft chorale across that mineral waste to darkness bearing lost to all history and all remembrance like a grail the sum of their secular and transitory and violent lives..."(5).(...)

More than a mere newly minted version of the romantic treatment of nature in fiction, in which landscape reflects the emotion of the characters. McCarthy's land and sky scape form an exterior version of the main characters' inner universe. And vice versa. We understand this more clearly in another passage offering us a glimpse of the night sky rather early in John Grady's flight into Mexico.

> He lay on his back in his blankets and looked out where the quartermoon lay cocked over the heel of the mountains. In that false blue dawn the Pleiades seemed to be rising up into the darkness above the world and dragging all the stars away, the great diamond of Orion and Cepella and the signature Cassiopeia all rising up through the phosphorous dark like a sea-net. He lay a long time listening to the others breathing in their sleep while he contemplated the wildness about him, the wildness within. (60)

"The wildness about him, the wildness within." That phrase suggests a certain geographical representation of psyche and natural world, with John Grady considering himself as a being possessing an inner nature who is embedded in a natural world of similar feel and texture. Holding inner and outer world in balance is McCarthy's prose, as represented in that phrase by the balancing comma.

The passage in which that phrase appears comes on a night just after John Grady and his companions Lacey Rawlins and the outlaw-in-training Jimmy Blevins have crossed the border into Mexico. There are few striking references to the landscape until they ride further south in the following day. But by early evening of that day they look to the north and see a rising storm front.

> ... all the sky to the north had darkened and the spare terrain they trod had turned a neuter gray as far as the eye could see. They grouped in the road at the top of a rise and looked back. The storm front towered above them and the wind was cool on their sweating faces. They slumped bleary-eyed in their saddles and looked at one another. Shrouded in the black thunderheads the distant lightning glowed mutely like welding seen through foundry smoke. As if repairs were under way at some flawed place in the iron dark of the world. (67)

As if shut off from an immediate return along the way they have come by this massive storm, the three adventurous boys proceed ever southward, encountering minor dangers until an escapade with a stolen horse leads Jimmy Blevins to launch a criminal foray in a small desert village for which all the boys take the blame. To escape they ride south and west through hill country toward a region they have heard of from a group of peasants they met in a desert; a lush section of farms against the western mountains in the state of Coahuila. Climbing the hills the next day they catch their first glimpse of this fabled terrain.

The grasslands lay in a deep violet haze and to the west thin flights of waterfowl were moving north before the sunset in the deep red galleries under the cloudbanks like schoolfish in a burning sea and on the foreland plain they saw vaqueros driving cattle before them through a gauze of golden dust. (93)

The land before him holds much promise for John Grady Cole, for his imminent education as a breaker of horses and prodigal son, as a boy turned man by means of love and tested by imprisonment and the blade. Readers who push forward through this provocatively biblical and lush and chiaroscuro mystery about one young Texan's growth of soul will find that the land is more than promising. The Mexico that rises up before us in the subsequent sections of the novel is, as Paz argues about the Mexico of Lawrence, Lowry and Rulfo, not so much a visionary landscape as a landscape of vision. The land is the promise, the promise is the land; alive, a symbol, a voice, a character; the book itself.

Vereen M. Bell on "Between the Wish and the Thing the World Lies Waiting"

McCarthy's symbols are never less than artfully naive, and their simplicity allows the reader to bear in mind that though this is a boy's story—in a richer but similarly ironic way that Huckleberry Finn is—it is deeply serious about the uncomplicated, romantic values that the boy's point of view keeps before us. We are not encouraged by the slightest inflection of the style to look upon John Grady and his friends with amusement or condescension. John Grady's youthfulness, and its associated idealism, is a correlative in itself—less a point of view than a private *episteme*, and one that refuses to be diminished. It is challenged persuasively both by experience and by a compelling history lesson in which John Grady is set straight by Alejandra's protective great-aunt; but it is never quite undone and we are not meant to think that it should be.

The Dueña Alfonsa, Alejandra's great-aunt, is friendly toward and admires John Grady, but in the end she opposes him as a suitor for her niece not because he is of the wrong class or nationality or because he is penniless but, in effect, because his luck is bad—or more precisely because he has not been hardened in the ways that would give him more control over his—and by extension Alejandra's—destiny. The old woman's agenda is pragmatic and revolutionary and—allowing for the culture she speaks through and against—resolutely feminist:

> Society is very important in Mexico. Where women do not even have the vote. In Mexico they are mad for society and for politics and very bad at both. My family are considered gachupines here, but the madness of the Spaniard is not so different from the madness of the Creole. The political tragedy in Spain was rehearsed in full dress twenty years earlier on Mexican soil. For those with eyes to see. Nothing was the same and yet everything. In the Spaniard's heart is a great yearning for freedom, but only his own. A great love of truth and

honor in all its forms, but not in its substance. And a deep conviction that nothing can be proven except that it be made to bleed. Virgins, bulls, men. Finally God himself.

Her own history encapsulates the horror and pathos of Mexico's history and because of that—because her story is a version of her culture's story—she has learned that the greatest tragedy is the cowardice of self-betrayal, and that self-betrayal occurs when one permits oneself to be diverted from the truth:

It may be that the life I desire for her no longer exists, yet I know what she does not. That there is nothing to lose. In January I will be seventy-three years old. I have known a great many people in that time and few of them led lives that were satisfactory to them. I would like for my grand-niece to have the opportunity to make a very different marriage from the one which her society is bent upon demanding of her. I wont accept a conventional marriage for her. Again, I know what she cannot. That there is nothing to lose. I dont know what sort of world she will live in and I have no fixed opinions concerning how she should live in it. I only know that if she does not come to value what is true above what is useful it will make little difference whether she lives at all. And by true I do not mean what is righteous but merely what is so.

In this respect, for the old woman, no matter how courageous and honorable he might be otherwise, John Grady is danger-ously unfinished. "In the end," she says, "we all come to be cured of our sentiments. Those whom life does not cure, death will. The world is quite ruthless in selecting between the dream and the reality, even when we will not. Between the *wish* and the *thing* the world lies waiting." This long Conradian mono-logue is presented through dramatic writing as chilling and as resonant as anything McCarthy has yet achieved.

The Dueña Alfonsa's position in John Grady's story brings to the foreground its profoundest irony. The ruling desire of McCarthy's strongest characters, from Arthur Ownby in *The*

Orchard Keeper to Cornelius Suttree in *Suttree*, is to live in some place that is not yet touched by the complications of the modern world, where it is possible to be one with the earth and to live in a genuine human communion. In practice this means that they want not so much to reverse history as to transcend it. It is no coincidence that when Cornelius Suttree is leaving Tennessee for the last time he stands above a roadbed where the new Knoxville expressway system is being built, connecting to the interstate system that will cause towns to die and cities to become indistinguishable. It is also no coincidence that he sees himself momentarily reflected and reclaimed in the blue eyes of a boy who has climbed the embankment to offer him water from a tin dipper.

John Grady Cole is Arthur Ownby in another time at a different age and also that reflection of himself younger that Suttree is permitted to see. Until now, in 1949, his grandfather's 18,000-acre cattle ranch has insulated him from history, but now that it is to be sold from around him, he can see the future coming. "People don't feel safe no more," his father says to him. "We're like the Comanches was two hundred years ago. We don't know what's goin to show up here come daylight. We don't even know what color they'll be." The father has given up, but John Grady is not waiting around to find out, and this is why he and Rawlins set out on horseback—how else?—meaning, without thinking or saying it in so many words, to move back in history by riding south. The great irony, as Señorita Alfonsa's story underscores, is that some kind of history is everywhere. The boys are too young to understand this yet (and many novelists and poets who should know better still don't): that there is no human place outside of time, and where human places are there are also the constructs and institutional artifacts of history. The fleas come with the dog. John Grady and Rawlins escape for a time the dissociating effects of the technology and capital of the new American order, but what they get from their adopted ancient culture is an attractive but totalitarian hierarchy—the autocratic rule of families, at best, and at worst, of brute power instead of law. In Enlightenment terms, a dignified ancient culture is also, inescapably, a primitive one.

It is not difficult at all to lapse into thinking of this story as taking place in the nineteenth century, or even earlier. The occasional battered truck and an especially ominous plane are surrealistically incongruous. John Grady and Rawlins bring an uncomplicated if wary democratic spirit into this old world which the system is unwilling to accommodate—itself stranded between past and future. What promises to be a dialectic turns out to be unproductive. What the outcome might have been imagined to be is, in the end, beside the point, for as the Dueña Alfonsa says, in history there are no control groups—there is nothing but what happens—and her own paradigmatic reading of history is grounded in the authentic tragedy of Francisco Madero's rise and fall—a story for her for all time of what results when intellectual idealism and political reality collide.

The story of Madero (his brother had been a suitor of Señorita Alfonsa's) seems to be a paradigm for McCarthy as well. There can be no doubt by now that McCarthy is a genuine—if somehow secular—mystic. This novel along with *Blood Meridian* shows him to be also a serious student of history, and that he reads history's lessons clearheadedly without the slightest chance of projecting politically correct or utopian back-formations upon it. His project is like Conrad's Marlow's, to continue to be able to believe in a numinous value at the heart of existence while remaining wholly without reassurance about this project from the realities of political life. Nor are there any practical hopes that what we can imagine in our moments of concentrated intuition has any chance at all of flourishing in the institutions—using the term advisedly—of men. In his writing, too, McCarthy must therefore always wrestle with the deconstructive angel, seeking to represent in mere words the "resonance ... like music ... which is the world itself" while knowing full well that language and music cannot be the same and that to try to represent this presence through a medium which is hopelessly grounded in material nature is to fail, and that to fail in this dedicated way is to enact, yet again—a human fractal—the whole problem in itself of being in the world.

So as a writer McCarthy's story is exactly the same as John Grady Cole's, except in a different time. John Grady in turn is clearly intended to be a saint of this project, and humorous and ordinary as he is at one level, he is inhumanly demanding at another, both of the world and of himself. When he reconnoiters with Rawlins back in Texas for the last time, his friend tries halfheartedly to talk him into staying on, maybe going to work on the oil rigs where the money's good. "This is still good country," he says. "Yeah. I know it is," John Grady says. "But it ain't my country." "What is your country," says Rawlins. "I don't know," John Grady says. "I don't know where it is. I don't know what happens to country." So he rides on out, as each unaccommodated visionary must inevitably do. Riding on in McCarthy's world gets to be a habit. His characters remain both medieval and irredeemably American.

NELL SULLIVAN ON MALE DESIRE

Each novel in the trilogy ultimately excludes the potentially significant female characters as part of a process of the obviation of women. Some forty years ago, Leslie Fiedler described the classic American novel as featuring a "strategy of evasion" of heterosexuality, because heterosexuality leads inexorably "to the fall to sex, marriage, and responsibility" (xx–xxi). While Robert Jarrett notes that the trilogy's commercial appeal is based in part on "significant elements of heterosexual romance" (99), under this thin veneer is a very different kind of love story, one much more consistent with Fiedler's *hierogamos* (or sacred marriage), "the peculiar American form of innocent homosexuality" (Fiedler 349, 531). Jarrett's recognition that John Grady Cole and Billy Parham experience "a loss of an initially stable identity based on a mythicized past" (105) might be extended, or rather, refined to reveal one facet of that loss: the destabilization of gender roles in the context of a Western narrative, in which gender roles are usually very clearly defined. While women are systematically eliminated from the narrative in the trilogy, the feminine itself remains and is ultimately "performed" by biologically-male characters. (...)

A merely cursory reading of Cormac McCarthy's novels reveals an unmistakable ambivalence about women, even an outright misogyny, manifested in the objectification of women as dead bodies in *Child of God* (1973), as the one-dimensional stereotypes witch, virgin, or whore in *Suttree* (1979), or as absence itself in much of *All the Pretty Horses* (1992) and *The Crossing* (1994). Particularly telling is McCarthy's turning from southern gothic novels to the Western, a genre which contemporary critics such as Tompkins and Lee Clark Mitchell recognize as a reaction against feminism and female authority (Mitchell 152; Tompkins, West 39–40).

All the Pretty Horses begins with John Grady Cole's betrayal by the two most important women in his life, his mother and his girlfriend, but the narrative soon avenges him. When his mother fails to register at the Menger Hotel under her married name and is escorted by a man other than his father, John Grady has no further contact with her. At the end of the novel, Lacey Rawlins asks if he has seen her, and he replies simply, "No" (298). He abjures his mother again in *Cities of the Plain* when Billy, hinting that John Grady might acquire the money to go to veterinary school from her, asks if John Grady ever writes her. Here, his response is a little more telling: "What's my mother got to do with anything?" (*COP* 217). Mary Catherine Barnett is not merely excluded, but visually contained at their final parting. John Grady sees no tears of remorse in her eyes, and when she offers her hand in farewell, he does not "know what she was doing" because he has "never shaken hands with a woman before" (*APH* 29). The narrative then encloses her within a "frame" so that she may never again exceed her proper limits:

> He stood back and touched the brim of his hat and turned and went on up the street. He didnt look back but he could see her in the windows of the Federal Building across the street standing there and she was *still* standing there when he reached the corner and stepped out of the glass forever. (29, emphasis added)

The implication is clear: John Grady steps out of the glass, moving beyond the moment, while Mary Catherine remains frozen there forever.

Even the women for whom John Grady retains affection are dispatched. Alejandra, who might be considered the second most important character in the novel if it is viewed as a traditional heterosexual love story, rides into the narrative on a horse and leaves on a train without much fanfare (John Grady works harder to reclaim his horse Redbo than to convince Alejandra to marry him). Abuela, who never really makes an appearance in the novel, is buried in "the unmarked earth" at the end of the novel; as John Grady stands tearfully at her grave, her chief value is revealed: "she had known and cared for the wild Grady boys" (*APH* 301). (...)

We learn early in *All the Pretty Horses* that the Grady men all die manly, that is, violent deaths. And so it will be for John Grady Cole, the last of the Grady men, who himself dies at the hand of another "serious man" (*COP* 198). Nonetheless, the same gender anxiety that besets Billy eventually creeps into McCarthy's characterization of John Grady Cole as well.

John Grady's status as the superior male is established early in *All the Pretty Horses*. Hearing John Grady's plans to go to Mexico, Lacey Rawlins asks, "If I dont go will you go anyways?" But John Grady is "already gone" (27), so Lacey follows him. Don Héctor is surprised to learn that Lacey is actually older than John Grady because John Grady is so clearly "the leader" (114). When Lacey fears for his life in prison, John Grady sternly orders him not to give up, sprinkling his pep-talk with several paternal *clichés*, "You listen to me," "You hear me?" and "I know it and I dont care" (182–83)—This leadership dynamic also exists between John Grady and Blevins, whom John Grady protects with the same paternal gruffness: "Do like I told you," he tells the slow-moving Blevins when danger is imminent (77). (...)

Like the "all-american cowboy" that he is, John Grady abides by the cowboy's code of silence. In *All the Pretty Horses*, a man commends John Grady's silence as "a good trait to have" (19). When Mary Catherine suggests they could remain friends, John Grady says contemptuously, "It's just talk, Mary Catherine" (28). And just as Boyd refuses to communicate with Billy, John Grady eventually shuts Lacey out, deferring, perhaps indefinitely, a discussion of the events at Saltillo: "I'll tell you. Let's just sit here. Let's not talk. Let's just sit here real quiet," John Grady tells Lacey, later repeating, "Let's just sit here real quiet" (208). The lack of verbal communication is part of his general affective reticence. (...)

More telling than the lack of tears is perhaps the sheer volume of blood that John Grady loses in the Border Trilogy. Like Billy Parham, he experiences vicarious menstruation, but the implications of this bleeding vary drastically between *All the Pretty Horses* and *Cities of the Plain*. Gail Kern Paster notes the connection between dramatic representations of bleeding and menstruation: "The bleeding body signifies as a shameful token of uncontrol, as a failure of physical self-mastery particularly associated with woman in her monthly 'courses'" (92). Twice in *All the Pretty Horses* John Grady suffers wounds that cause his boots to fill with blood (202, 268). His boots "sloshed" and his clothes "sagged with the weight of the blood" after the knife-fight in prison (201). After being shot in the thigh, his "trousers were dark with blood and there was blood on the ground" (266), and later the captive captain notes the wound, which is "still bleeding" (272). But in this scene, the anxiety surrounding male blood loss is abated because even in displaying the feminine, John Grady manages to display the phallic at the same time. As the captain looks on in disbelief, John Grady cauterizes his thigh wound with his own pistol by "jamm[ing] the redhot barrel ash and all down into the hole in his leg" (274). (...)

In her study of male homosocial desire, Eve Kosofsky Sedgwick posits "a continuum between homosocial and homosexual—a continuum whose visibility, for men, in our society, is radically disrupted" (1–2). Desire appears in many guises along the male homosocial continuum, but always as "the affective or social force, the glue, even when its manifestation is hostility or hatred or something less emotively charged, that shapes an important relationship" (2). (...)

While it is true that genital sexuality is not a component of the relationship between the two men, there is an undeniable cathexis of desire between them; such palpable desire between a man and a woman would certainly be labeled sexual even if it were never consummated. (...)

This homoerotic longing is evident in the verbal and nonverbal expressions of jealousy so prevalent in the trilogy. Lacey is jealous not only of Alejandra, but of Blevins, as is evident when he advocates leaving Blevins behind. When John Grady asks how Lacey would feel if it were he, Lacey replies, "I wouldnt leave you and you wouldnt leave me. That aint no argument," implying that the bond between John Grady and himself should exclude Blevins (*APH* 79). His feelings of betrayal are clear when he refuses to meet John Grady's eyes after the two are arrested (153). (...)

Lacey Rawlins' more demure expression occurs when he sings, "Will you miss me, will you miss me. Will you miss me when I'm gone" (*APH* 37), a musical version of his earlier question, "If I dont go will you go anyways?" (27), or more simply, how much do you love me? At the end of the novel, he discovers the answer when John Grady rebuffs his offer of comfortable domesticity, "You could stay here at the house" (299). (...)

With its destabilization of gender identity, the Border Trilogy could be regarded as McCarthy's most subversive work. Yet, while male performance of the feminine seemingly undermines the notion of "natural" male domination, it also becomes one more strategy to contain feminine power and obviate women. As feminist theorist Tania Modleski notes, men "deal with the threat of female power by incorporating it.... [M]ale power frequently works to efface female subjectivity by occupying the site of femininity" (7). In this sense, the gender trouble experienced by the trilogy's boys may be yet another symptom of McCarthy's narrative misogyny: the text of male desire appropriating the feminine while perpetually striving to make women themselves unnecessary. (...)

However, McCarthy undercuts even this grudging inclusion by carefully constructing a paradigm of desire as a masculine *cul-de-sac*, a paradigm that demands the systematic expulsion of women from the narrative.

PHILLIP A. SNYDER ON COWBOY CODES

Operating in the midst of the twentieth century and endangered by habitat loss and familial dislocation, McCarthy's cowboys must adapt to a new western environment or die, particularly after their attempts to relocate themselves in Mexico, the original, centuries-old site of cowboying in the Americas, prove to be instructive and evocative but ultimately unsuccessful. Although unrivaled in its stylistic excellence and thematic complexity, the Border Trilogy shares with other modern and contemporary western texts a hard-edged nostalgia for the cowboy past tinged with a persistent advocation of cowboy virtues in the present, particularly as invested in the materiality of cowboy culture. (...)

To sustain its exploration of the ambiguous space between the myth and reality of the modern West, the Border Trilogy depends primarily on its two young protagonists, both of whom possess a visceral loyalty to a vanishing lifestyle and a stubborn persistence in guest completion. *All the Pretty Horses* chronicles sixteen-year-old John Grady Cole's 1948 American disinheritance and his subsequent Mexican search to recover the familial ranching dream from which he has been and will continue to be distanced. (...)

Thus McCarthy critiques and renovates, at the same time as he reaffirms the cowboy wiles which structure the behavioral patterns of John Grady and Billy. These cowboy codes also embody ideals which signify well beyond their western borders, reflecting national notions of a fundamental American identity and revealing an essentially American anxiety over the apparent instability of that identity. As Henry Nash Smith observes in *Virgin Land* with reference to Frederick Jackson Turner's frontier thesis, Americans may still see themselves as having been formed by the call of the West and the requirements of extending the border between civilization and frontier westward across the country. Writing around the same time period in which the Border Trilogy is set, Smith calls this frontier notion a "massive and deeply held conviction" (4), and it remains a pervasive cultural myth today regardless of its historical validity. In short, we, along with John Grady and Billy, want to believe in the pragmatic sufficiency of a mythic ideology. This may be the most significant border McCarthy explores in the trilogy—the one that lies in the gap between the ideal and the real, a wild zone in which often conflicting elements are given play to produce a shifting relation of theory and practice: characterized by a deferral of closure and marked by a continuous accommodation. (...)

Accordingly, McCarthy's articulation of cowboy codes eschews closed interpretations of simplistic singularity and instead celebrates their function as open dialogic figures capable of suggesting an ambient and infinite signification within the gaps present in even their most essential aspects. McCarthy's cowboy codes may be represented productively as binary figures—such as independence/integration for the paradoxical cowboy character—whose deconstruction produces borderline meanings which subvert, rather than assert, the code's hegemonic hierarchy. (...)

While we may structure many such possible figures, the following five binary codes will suffice to demonstrate the basic status of cowboy codes in the Border Trilogy as essentially heterogeneous and thus ethically grounded independence/integration, dominance/dependence, rivalry/respect, survival/hospitality, and actions/eloquence. (...)

Independence/Integration. (...)

The judgment of others is only one aspect of John Grady's self–other relationships that figures predominantly in the novel; the self's call to responsibility for the other may be far more significant. Jimmy Blevins, for example, the lightning-spooked boy outlaw who wants to join in with John Grady and Lacey Rawlins in Mexico "Cause I'm an American" (45), represents more than a test of John Grady's pragmatism; rather, Blevins represents a test of John Grady's ethics and his willingness to take responsibility for the other, however troublesome or guilty or destructive or evil Blevins may turn out to be. Further, John Grady does not have a choice between naïvete and maturity, or between romance and reality in accepting responsibility for Blevins; rather, his choice is between enacting his idealistic cowboy codes or not, for these codes leave meaning only as they are enacted within a communal context in the real world. While Rawlins rightly predicts dire consequences from their association with Blevins and justifiably says, "I aint taken no responsibility for him" (69), John Grady simply says, "I dont believe I can leave him out here afoot" (71), even though Blevins—near-naked and horseless—is entirely responsible for his own predicament. The notion of partnership, even their marginal one with Blevins, pervades the novel for good and for ill: paradoxically, it not only saves John Grady and Rawlins in prison as they fight together for survival because they use the money Blevins slips them just before his execution for necessary bribes, but it also attaches them to Blevins and his guilt, which attachment puts them into prison in the first place. (...)

Dominance/Dependence. (...)

John Grady in particular illustrates this ethical joining up of cowboy and house in his repeated demonstrations of his "natural horsemanship," ranging from his amazing feats of riding to his unwillingness to turn on the barn light at night because it "bothers the horses" (*Cities* 41). McCarthy establishes this cowboy/horse connection as a fundamental motif in the trilogy early on as he describes John Grady and his father taking their last ride together:

> The boy who rode on slightly before him sat a horse not only is if he'd been born to it which he was but as if were he begot by malice or mischance into some queer land where horses never were he would have found them anyway. Would have known that there was something missing for the world to be right or he right in it and would have set forth to wander wherever it was needed for as long as it took until he came upon one and he would have known that that was what he sought and it would have been. (*APH* 23)

Here McCarthy undercuts the ubiquitous nature-or-nurture conundrum by his double simile which, while giving a brief acknowledgment to nurture in John Grady's cowboy identity ("as if he'd been born to it which he was"), develops around a hypothetical proposition to give nature more than its just due ("he would have known that that was what he sought"). Nevertheless, neither nature nor nurture dominates here but are mutually dependent, incomplete without the other, just as John Grady would have been incomplete without horses. The final passage of the novel further reflects this absolute integration of cowboy and horse as John Grady rides off into the sunset with Redbo and the Blevins bay horse: "horse and rider and horse passed on and their long shadows passed in tandem like the shadow of a single being" (301). Although McCarthy describes the relationship between John Grady and horses as almost mystical, he keeps that relation grounded in reality and refuses either to anthropomorphize horses or make John Grady a part of the horse herd; he and horses may have a relationship, but they remain discrete and disassociated. For example, when John Grady is breaking the wildest horse in *La Purísima*'s string, a "bucketheaded ... grullo" (105), to demonstrate the practical effectiveness of his horse-breaking ideology to a skeptical Rawlins, his success depends not on domination or identification, but on relation. In reply to Rawlins's question regarding the efficacy of "sacking out" the horse before saddling it to familiarize it with being touched, John Grady responds, "I dont know.... I aint a horse" (106), emphasizing his unwillingness to subsume the horse within the self, or the other within the same, by pretending he understands what a horse thinks or feels. (...)

Rivalry/Respect. (...)

The most significant exchanges in McCarthy often occur between enemies.

In *All the Pretty Horses*, for example, John Grady's relationship with Dueña Alfonsa turns on their respective love and concern for Alejandra which also sets them at odds with one another despite their obvious affinity and places John Grady both in and out of harm's way. Their chess games serve as an obvious symbolic counterpart to their conversations, which fluctuate continuously along the rivalry/respect border and reflect the Dueña's superiority in determining the most effective overall strategy and in pursuing the chess moves it generates. In their early conversations, as in their early chess games, she measures John Grady's discourse skills in much the same way as the unnamed prison assassin and the pimp Eduardo later measure his knife-fighting skills, so that she can ascertain how best to checkmate him rhetorically. She concludes their first conversation by making clear exactly what is at issue and who determines it, refuting John Grady's appeal to justice: "No. It's not a matter of right. You must understand. It is a matter of who must say. In this matter I get to say. I am the one who gets to say" (137). She concludes their second conversation, which includes a long autobiographical account of her life remarkable for its intimate detail, by making clear exactly what constitutes their relationship: "I've been at some pains to tell you about myself because among other reasons I think we should know who our enemies are" (240–41). (...)

Survival/Hospitality. (...)

Instances of hospitality abound throughout the Border Trilogy, particularly in the first two volumes, as multiple manifestations of its dominant motif: the wandering stranger being taken in and cared for. In *All the Pretty Horses*, John Grady is picked up every time he tries to hitch a ride regardless of the weather or other circumstances; he, Rawlins, and Blevins are taken ill, fed, put up overnight, and packed a lunch the next day by a family at a small *estancia* who refuse any payment; two girls get them cigarettes at their request when they are prisoners and cry about their probable fate; John Grady buys the knife that saves his life from his fellow prisoners, Faustino and the Sierra León Indian; and, after his escape, he is spared by three "Men of the country" (281) who, instead of robbing him of his goods and horses, give him a *serape* because he does not have one. (...)

Action/Eloquence. (...)

Although action and language signify equally well for McCarthy, behavioral performance may he privileged over verbal. In *All the Pretty Horses* John Grady differentiates between the values of "reasonable" discourse and loyal behavior in responding to Rawlins's I-told-you-so speech after they are arrested because of their association with Blevins: "I know you did [tried to reason with me.] But some things aint reasonable.... You either stick or you quit and I wouldnt quit you I dont care what you dome" (155–56). Later, when the captain tries to undermine his story, he says, "There aint but one truth.... The truth is what happened. It aint what come out of somebody's mouth" (168).

TOM PILKINGTON ON FATE AND FREE WILL ON THE AMERICAN FRONTIER

On the surface the plot of *All the Pretty Horses* appears a variation on a story that has been told often in western literature. A wandering cowboy and his sidekick ride innocently into hostile territory. There ensue fights against insurmountable odds, the hero's romance with a lovely young señorita, chases on horseback through a harsh but beautiful landscape. Readers understand quickly enough, however, that this simple tale is but the vehicle on which they are to be taken on an excursion into the complex realms of philosophy.

First, we must consider the horses. John Grady and his pal Lacey Rawlins love horses more than anything else. When they get jobs at La Purísima hacienda in Coahuila working with wild horses, they are pleased as can be. At one point John Grady observes the mustangs running in circles in their corral "like marbles swirled in a jar." Compare this description with Faulkner's in "Spotted Horses": "we could watch them spotted varmints swirling along the fence and back and forth across the lot same as minnows in a pond."

For both Faulkner and McCarthy, horses are more incorporeal spirits than they are creatures of blood and bone. Faulkner's horses are malign; they are swarming Furies, sent by the gods to punish men for their folly. McCarthy's horses, however, represent the vital life force of the universe. They stand for what is, pristine and unfallen nature in its most elemental form.

On several occasions John Grady dreams of horses:

In his sleep he could hear the horses stepping among the rocks ... and in his sleep he dreamt of horses and the horses in his dream moved gravely among the tilted stones like horses come upon an antique site where some ordering of the world had failed and if anything had been written on the stones the weathers had taken it away again and the horses were wary and moved with great circumspection carrying in their blood as they did the recollection of this and other places where horses once had been and would be again. Finally what he saw in his dream was that the order in the horse's heart was more durable for it was written in a place where no rain could erase it.

The old *mozo* Luís tells John Grady that "the horse shares a common soul and its separate life only forms it out of all horses and makes it mortal. He said that if a person understood the soul of the horse then he would understand all horses that ever were." But according to Luís, "among men there was no such communion as among horses." The singularity and the problems of humanity, Luís implies, stem from individual human consciousness. Only humans, of all earth's creatures, contemplate abstractions like truth and justice. Only humans are capable of viciousness, perfidy, evil. Only humans aspire— futilely—to build empires and lasting monuments, among the ruins of which horses contentedly graze.

All the Pretty Horses is, on one level, a coming-of-age story. John Grady is sixteen when the tale begins. It is in adolescence, of course, that the issues of free will and fate are raised with greatest poignancy. In order for the young herself to achieve a secure sense of identity, he or she must resolve the conflict between pressures from family and his or her desire for freedom and autonomy. (...)

Whatever else he may be, John Grady in the beginning is an American—a *norteamericano*. He believes in individualism, free will, volition. He thinks that every man born on this planet is an Adam, free of memory and external constraint, able to shape his illimitable "self" in any way he chooses. He is shocked when Alejandra refuses to break all ties to go with him.

Which is the dominant agent—free will or late? Perhaps there is no either-or answer. In her final—rather improbable—conversation with John Grady, Alfonsa argues for a kind of modified predestination. The conditions of the physical universe impose certain conditions on the individual, including total unpredictability. But life is a shimmering web, and every time a strand is struck by the assertion of will, the web vibrates with consequences for all. Actually Alfonsa uses the metaphor of puppets. If one looks behind the curtain at the puppet show, she says, one finds puppets who control puppets who control puppets and on to infinity. There is, in other words, a vast interconnectedness of things, so that clear causal relationships are impossible to isolate.

By novel's end John Grady has fashioned a code to live by. It is a code of honor and responsibility—à la Hemingway—that has nothing to do with legality or traditional morality. It is an internal code and has been shaped by hard experience and the hard conditions of an indifferent universe.

The scene in the hotel room in Zacatecas—John Grady and Alejandra's last night together—is crucial. "He saw very clearly how all his life led only to this moment and all after led nowhere at all. He felt something cold and soulless enter him like another being and he imagined that it smiled malignly and he had no reason to believe that it would ever leave him." He immediately is invaded by what the Spanish call *la tristesa de la vida*: "He imagined the pain of the world to be like some form-less parasitic being seeking out the warmth of human souls wherein to incubate and he thought he knew what made one liable to its visitations." (...)

John Grady's seemingly capricious decision to return to Encantada to recover his and Lacey Rawlins's horses, which have been appropriated by a local *hacendado*, may he seen as an attempt to impose order and justice on a world in which there is no inherent order or justice. It is also a direct response to what has happened in Zacatecas—a near-suicidal statement of grief and disillusionment. It symbolizes the lifting of the world's sorrows onto his own shoulders. He never will be a naive innocent again.

As is true of all McCarthy's fiction, *All the Pretty Horses* contains plenty of riveting action, including a knife fight in a Mexican prison in which John Grady kills a man. Back in Texas, John Grady wanders over the countryside, like a young Ancient Mariner, compulsively explaining to whomever will listen why he had killed his fellow inmate. In Mexico, John Grady accepted the act without much thought; it seemed fated, part of a predetermined destiny. In the U.S.—the land of freedom—accountability and responsibility are the necessary complements of free will and volition.

Edwin T. Arnold on Dreams and Visions

All the Pretty Horses begins with John Grady Cole viewing his grandfather's corpse. "That was not sleeping," he thinks. "That was not sleeping" (3). John Grady here, probably unconsciously, alludes to and contradicts both Jesus, who says of Jarius's daughter, "The child is not dead but sleeping" (Mark 5.39; see also Matt. 9.24 and Luke 9.52) and Prince Hamlet's meditation: "To die, to sleep; / sleep: perchance to dream" (*Hamlet*, 3. 1. 64–65). If he has read Shakespeare, then perhaps he recognizes the similarity between Hamlet's situation and his own.[15] He is roused to action not by the ghost of his father, but by another spectral vision "like a dream of the past," that of the "lost nation ... out of the north," the "nation and ghost of nation passing in a soft chorale" along the old Comanche road (5). This passage describes a thing both ancient and other-worldly, and yet McCarthy suggests that the vision is not imagined by the boy or present to him only. Indeed, even after John Grady "must turn the pony up onto the plain and homeward," the "warriors would ride on in that darkness they'd become, rattling past with their stone-age tools of war in default of all substance and singing softly in blood and longing south across the plains to Mexico" (6). The vision, then, exists independent of the boy—these ghostly figures out of the past are still a very real part of the world, whether seen or not, whether "alive" or not. At this moment the boy has the eyes and the spirit to witness them, but they do not depend on his witnessing for their existence. By the end of the book, he himself will become a similar vision, witnessed by the descendants of this "lost nation," who "stood and watched him pass and watched him vanish upon that landscape solely because he was passing. Solely because he would vanish" (301). Since John Grady is moving toward death (and also toward legend) throughout the trilogy, this is an apt and appropriate conclusion (with more than a few similarities to the ending of *Suttree* as well).

But the John Grady we meet at the beginning of *All the Pretty Horses* is still a sixteen-year-old boy with hopes and aspirations, motivated by romantic ideas. The first pages of the novel comprise an extended leavetaking of home, parents, girlfriend; then John Grady, reflected in the window of the San Angelo Federal Building, like Alice "stepped out of the glass forever" (29) and into another world. The episodes that make up this first chapter reveal John Grady and Rawlins's naïvete and good hearts, but they also plant the seeds for the tragedies that will follow. By the end of the chapter, the boys are deep in the Mexican state of Coahuila, hired to work as hands on the fabulous *Hacienda de Nuestra Señora de la Purísima Concepción*. They have seen Don Héctor Rocha y Villareal's daughter Alejandra, and John Grady has begun to fantasize of a life—with her on this magnificent ranch, a miraculous replacement for the family and land he has lost back in Texas. The chapter ends with Rawlins talking to John Grady as they lie in their bunks. "This is some country, aint it?" Rawlins says. "Yeah. It is," John Grady answers. "Go to sleep." "This is how it was with the old waddies, aint it?" Lacey persists. "How long do you think you'd like to stay here?" "About a hundred years," John Grady replies. "Go to sleep" (96).

Chapter 2 might very easily be read as an extended dream experienced in that sleep. Obviously we are not meant to take this possibility literally—the events that tallow are "real" in the world of the novel—but the boys' experiences at the *hacienda* do comprise the kind of adolescent fantasy found in youthful adventure tales. Some have criticized the book for exactly this quality, the unlikeliness of it all, but that may be the point of the tale. After all, the title of the book comes from a lullaby in which the baby is being sung to sleep with the promise that "When you wake, / You shall have / All the pretty little horses."[16] The boys have not yet been mastered by the world, wakened to its harshness, although John Grady has been warned by his dying father of this inevitability during their last conversation. "We're like the Comanches was two hundred years ago. We dont know what's goin to show up here come daylight. We dont even know what color they'll be" (25–26), he says, almost as if he, too, had once shared his son's vision of the ghostly tribe.[17]

Don Héctor's ranch is edenic—"In the lakes and in the streams were species of fish not known elsewhere on earth and birds and lizards and other forms of life as well all long relict here for the desert stretched away on every side" (97).[18] Here John Grady has moments of transcendence in which the earth itself becomes an animate being, like the horses he rides: "he lay looking up at the stars in their places and the hot belt of matter that ran the chord of the dark vault overhead and he put his hands on the ground at either side of him and pressed them against the earth and in that coldly burning canopy of black he slowly turned dead center to the world, all of it taut and trembling and moving enormous and alive under his hands" (119). His thoughts, however, are directed primarily on Alejandra, and it must be noted that the boy's dreams at this stage are focused on his own egotistical desires, his personal, physical passions. (...)

John Grady has experienced a delusional dream in this chapter, an intoxicating fantasy that has led him into danger and from which he must now extricate himself if he can. After their arrest, Lacey asks John Grady if he has tried to wake Don Héctor in order to make sense of the situation. When John Grady admits that he has not, Lacey informs him, "They said he was awake. They said he'd been awake for a long time. Then they laughed" (155). That Don Héctor has known the truth about the boys, and has perhaps suspected John Grady's relationship with his daughter, is appropriately expressed in terms of such wakefulness, and we now realize that the father has, in earlier conversations, cautioned the boy against the very (feeds John Grady subsequently commits.[20]

In jail he dreams of horses, of dream horses, variations of the "picture-book horses" in his grandfather's painting (16). This is also a dream of freedom, for he runs among them "in a field on a high plain" (161), and it is further a recognition of something more he finds in that "high world" and that is "a resonance that was like a music among them and they were none of them afraid horse nor colt nor mare and they ran in that resonance which is the world itself and which cannot be spoken but only praised" (161–62). Here we have an example of an experience beyond words—it "cannot be spoken but only praised." Here the dream offers the direct, unmediated moment, the physical, fundamental awareness of the world's "resonance." The term refers to the intensification or enrichment of a sound or feeling. In physics, it describes the effect one vibrating body has on another body: the movement of the first is translated to the second so that both bodies come to move together. In this sense, the transcendent wonder of the "high world" is transmitted through the medium of dream to the ordinary world in which the boy lives and provides him with momentary escape from the "detention center" in which he now finds himself. The resonance of the dream repeats a long-held McCarthy concept that all life is flux, that all being is energy, that, as we read in *Suttree*, "Nothing ever stops moving."[21]

Still later, in the Saltillo prison, John Grady knows that he must stay awake to survive. After he has been badly cut in the knife fight in which he kills his attacker, he finally does sleep and dreams of the dead, "standing about in their bones and the dark sockets of their eyes that were indeed without speculation bottomed in the void wherein lay a terrible intelligence common to all but of which none would speak" (205). Rawlins will later comment, "Dying aint in people's plans, is it?" (210); but from this point on John Grady comes to accept, and perhaps finally to desire, his death. Dreams as forms of visitation from the dead date at least to ancient Greek mythology and become a recurring trope in the Border Trilogy, in which the dead are never far from the living, whether historically—as in the constant social memories of the Mexican Revolution—or personally. When John Grady returns to *La Purísima* to retrieve both his belongings and, he fervently hopes, Alejandra herself, he "thought what sort of dream might bring him luck" and thinks to dream of the girl. Instead, before sleeping, he remembers a ghostly visitation while in the Saltillo prison by the murdered Jimmy Blevins, a time when "Blevins came to sit beside him and they talked of what it was like to be dead and Blevins said it was like nothing at all and he believed him." Blevins now replaces Alejandra in John Grady's dream, and, in fact, comes to negate her and any "luck" she might bring him: "He thought perhaps if he dreamt of him enough he'd go away forever and be dead among his kind and the grass scissored in the wind at his ear and he fell asleep and dreamt of nothing at all" (225). (...)

John Grady's last dream in the book is again one of horses, and it reveals, I think, a more mature acceptance of the tragic nature of the world. This time the horses do not run; rather they "moved gravely among the tilted stones like horses come upon in antique site where some ordering of the world had failed and if anything had been written on the stones the weathers had taken it away again...." A deeper order, however, resides in the horses' hearts, "a place where no rain could erase it" (280). (...)

Following this dream John Grady Cole becomes more aware of the mysterious workings of the world.

Notes

15. Jennifer Fraser has drawn a number of other similarities between John Grady and Hamlet in her unpublished essay "The Border Trilogy: McCarthy's Marriage of Figura."

16. Dianne C. Luce makes the point that the "pretty horses of the title come to represent any fantasy, dream, wish, or object of desire to which one might aspire or feel entitled to ..." (156). She also discusses John Grady's growth in terms of "waking" from a dream. ("'When you wake'" 155–67).

17. One might compare many of the previously-discussed passages to the view of the world described by William Faulkner in such works as *Go Down, Moses*, his meditation on man and nature, the world we know and the world sometimes revealed to us. In the section "The Old People," for example, Isaac McCaslin kills his first buck and "Sam Fathers marked his face with the hot blood which he had spilled and he ceased to be a child and became a hunter and a man" (132). Shortly thereafter Isaac sees what must he a phantom deer, the spirit of the woods. He tries to explain it to his cousin McCaslin Edmonds, and Cass responds. "Think of all that has happened here, on this earth. All the blood hot and strong for living, pleasuring, that has soaked back into it.... And all that must be somewhere; all that could not have been invented and created just to be thrown away. And the earth is shallow; there is not a great deal of it before you come to the rock. And the earth dont want to just keep things, hoard them; it wants to use them again." "But I saw it!" Isaac insists, fearing that Cass misunderstands the literalness of the event. "I saw him!" "Steady," Cass replies. "I know you did. So did I. Sam took me in there once after I killed my first deer" (138–39).

18. The *hacienda* is located "along the edge of the Bolsón de Cuatro Ciénagas in the state of Coahuila" (97). Despite the paradisiacal qualities, McCarthy's description of the basin is not exaggerated, for it is a unique geographical area and supports a variety of fish and other aquatic life forms not found elsewhere in the world. Much of the area is now under the management of the Nature Conservancy, which is attempting to protect the special quality of the region. I am grateful to Robert G. McCready, Northeast Mexico Program Manager of The Nature Conservancy of Texas (and a devoted reader of the Trilogy), for information concerning Cuatro Ciénagas.

20. See Christine Chollier's essay "Autotextuality, or Dialogic Imagination in Cormac McCarthy's Border Trilogy," in this collection for further discussion of Don Héctor's warnings.

21. A great deal is happening in this passage. As Dianne Luce pointed out to me, McCarthy here echoes in his vocabulary Dylan Thomas's "Fern Hill," in which the poet remembers being "green and carefree, famous among the barns / About the happy yard and singing as the farm. was home" (ll. 10–11). The poem continues:

> And then to awake, and the farm, like a wanderer white
> Will the dew, come back, the cock on his shoulder: it was all
> Shining,
> it was Adam and Maiden,
> The sky gathered again
> And the sun grew round that very day.
> So it must have been after the birth of the simple light
> In the first, spinning place, the spellbound horses walking warm
> Out of the whinnying green stable
> On to the fields of praise. (ll. 28–36)

"Fern Hill" is also alluded to in *Child of God*, in Lester's dream of his father and the heart-breaking beauty of the world (170–71). But the passage goes beyond Thomas's lyrical romanticism. In theoretical physics, the ongoing exploration into the structure of the world of subatomic particles posits a unified theory of the universe. This "theory of everything" now concentrates on "string theory," which holds that the smallest scales of material within the atom are "loops of vibrating string." As Brian Greene puts it in his book *The Elegant Universe*, "Far from being a collection of chaotic experimental facts, particle properties in string theory are the manifestation of one and the same physical feature: the resonant patterns of vibration—the music, so to speak—of fundamental loops of strings" (15–16).

MARK BUSBY ON CORMAC MCCARTHY'S BORDER CROSSINGS

Cormac McCarthy's Southwestern novels are tied together by the repetition of the powerful metaphor of border crossings. In the three novels of the Border Trilogy—*All the Pretty Horses, The Crossing,* and *Cities of the Plain*—McCarthy uses the border as a metaphor for a complex and oxymoronic melding of nihilism and optimism, good and evil, illusion and reality, and several similar contrasts. He also employs similar structural patterns to examine the complex intertwining of positive and negative forces to present ultimately a worldview that suggests a nihilistic optimism. (...)

The border, therefore, represents a line between such opposing forces as civilization/wilderness, individual/community, fate/free will, past/present, aggression/passivity and numerous others central to the Southwestern legend. This awareness of borders grows in intensity in the contemporary Southwest as the schism between old and new tears more strongly at the human heart. Increasingly, contemporary Southwestern writers such as McCarthy examine the sharp division between the frontier myth that lives inside and the diminished outside natural world fraught with complexity, suffering, and violence but leavened with humor, compassion, and love. What McCarthy adds to the older frontier formula is his use of 'la frontera,' the North/South border between the American Southwest and Northern Mexico, as the boundary line between warring forces. (...)

McCarthy, therefore, combines Southern, Southwestern, and Mexican history into a rich fiction that uses older American elements such as the story of the young boy's initiation as the basis. Each McCarthy novel takes a representative young boy's initiatory experience through a border crossing and turns the experience upside down so that the expected initiation is thwarted and seemingly denied. But ironically, it is through the denied experience that a young man is initiated into a more profound understanding than the expected initiation could have offered. Each novel focuses on a complex series of opposing forces, but each novel provides a different emphasis. While all three deal with reality/illusion, individual/community, linearity/circularity, home/not home, dispossession/possession, life/death, and father/son, *All the Pretty Horses* highlights the opposing forces of fate/free will, cowardice/courage, restriction/freedom, class/classlessness, time/timelessness, reason/imagination, order/chaos, master/slave, home/not home, and justice/injustice. (...)

John Grady's ultimate recognition of the limitation of self is one important aspect of the novel. Indeed the sharp contrast between the individual and community, between concern for self and concern for the other, is another one of the central conflicts. Faced with his grandfather's death, rejected by his girlfriend and his mother, supported weakly by an ineffectual father, John Grady replaces his broken family community with the comradeship of Lacey Rawlins, and this small community is broadened by chance when the irrepressible Jimmy Blevins joins them. Blevins forces John Grady to consider his responsibility for another, much to the pragmatic Rawlins' dismay. John Grady is initially led to these concerns when Blevins (pointing to another contrast—rationality/irrationality) crazily shucks his gun, horse, boots, and clothes out of his fear that he is fated to be struck by lightning ('I'm double bred for death by fire', 68). John Grady tells Rawlins: 'I dont believe I can leave him out there afoot' (71).

John Grady's strong feelings of responsibility for Blevins continue and expand after Blevins is executed in the woods by the captain. Haunted by his failure to act and only vaguely understanding his motives, John Grady makes a choice to pursue the captain in language that recalls probably the most famous moral decision in American literature, Huck Finn's famous conclusion, 'All right then, I'll go to hell', when he decides not to return Jim to slavery. Rejected by Alejandra, John Grady rides aimlessly until he reaches a crossroads. Sitting on his horse, he reads road signs and seeing the arrow to

La Encantada, he 'looked toward the darkness in west. The hell with it, he said. I aint leavin my horse down there' (257). Unlike Huck's clear decision, John Grady's is murky and unformed, and he only vaguely understands why he sets off to repossess his horse from the captain.

Later he feels compelled to tell his story to the judge, saying 'The reason I wanted to kill him was because I stood there and let him walk that boy out in the trees and shoot him and I never said nothin' (293). But in McCarthy's world good and evil are often intertwined, and John Grady must seek out the judge after the hearing to tell him, 'I guess what I wanted to say first of all was that it kindly bothered me in the court what you said. It was like I was in the right about everthing and I dont feel that way.' Instead, he says, 'I dont feel justified' (290). Ultimately, then, John Grady Cole's border crossing has taken him into a world of complexity, ambiguity, and ambivalence—a mixture of good and evil, rationality and irrationality, fate and free will in a mestizo culture that is itself an amalgam. Nowhere is the complex mixture more apparent than in John Grady's dealings with the Dueña Alfonsa, whose statements and personal history are belied by her actions. (...)

Ironically, it is Alfonsa, the former idealist, who most fully challenges John Grady's idealism, telling him: 'In the end we all come to be cured of our sentiments. Those whom life does not cure death will. The world is quite ruthless in selecting between the dream and the reality, even where we will not. Between the wish and the thing the world lies waiting' (238). (...)

This mixture of sadness and beauty is now part of John Grady's more intricate understanding of the world of responsibility to both humans and animals. On the way back to Texas he sees a wedding, a celebratory beginning that is tempered by the 'pale rider' as he passes (284). Very shortly after seeing the wedding, traditional ceremonial beginning, he attends the funeral of the woman who had worked for his family for fifty years:

he said goodbye to her in Spanish and then turned and put on his hat and turned his wet face to the wind and for a moment he held out his hands as if to steady himself or as if to bless the ground there or perhaps as if to slow the world that was rushing away and seemed to care nothing for the old or the young or rich or poor or dark or pale or he or she. Nothing for their struggles, nothing for their names. Nothing for the living or the dead. (301)

When John Grady rides off into the sunset at the end of this novel, it is not the optimistic triumph of the traditional Western. It is instead a complex image of how the 'rider and horse passed on and their long shadows passed in tandem like the shadow of a single being. Passed and paled into the darkening land, the world to come' (302).

Sara L. Spurgeon on Truth and Redemption

The icon of the sacred cowboy is one of our most potent national fantasies, visible in everything from blue jeans to car commercials to popular films. This mythic figure, however, like that of the hunter preceding it, is bound to crumble, for it is hollow at its core and stripped bare by McCarthy in *All the Pretty Horses*. As he slowly begins to recognize the fragility and falseness of his life, John Grady Cole seeks a return to the imagined innocence of the sacred cowboy of the mythic past. (...)

The life John Grady has been living on his family's Texas ranch is a romantic fantasy, ubiquitously familiar to every American through innumerable novels, films, grade school history texts, beer and cigarette advertisements. It is nonetheless a mask, a rose-colored and stereotyped cliché of the national symbolic barely hiding the falseness at its core. That this particular myth strides about on feet of clay is made apparent not just through the imminent sale of the ranch, but through the persistent return of all that this version of national fantasy attempts to deny and repress, the truth of its conception so brutally revealed in *Blood Meridian*. McCarthy lovingly evokes that myth and at the same time strips away the layers of fantasy that make belief in it possible.

The violent past thrusts itself into the present in *Pretty Horses* almost immediately, as the novel opens with John Grady leaving the funeral of his cowboy/rancher grandfather to ride

> the western fork of the old Comanche road coming down out of the Kiowa country .... the ancient road was shaped before him in the rose and canted light like a dream of the past where the painted ponies and the riders of that lost nation came down out of the north ... all of them pledged in blood and redeemable in blood only .... nation and ghost of nation passing in a soft chorale across that mineral waste to darkness bearing lost to all history and all remembrance like a grail the sum of their secular and transitory and violent lives. (5)

The very people scalped for profit in *Blood Meridian* to allow for white settlement—the nation made ghost so that generations of Gradys and Coles could run cattle—limn with darkness and blood the wholesome myth of that most privileged of western icons, the independent rancher. The vanished Comanches traverse the gap in the national symbolic left bare by this version of national fantasy that resolutely ignores the reality, the noninnocence, of its own history. They are "pledged in blood and redeemable in blood only," but so is the nation replacing them and riding the same trail, side by side with their ghosts. John Grady, in his innocent acceptance of the noninnocent myth of the sacred cowboy realizes only faintly this debt of blood, and not at all that it will fall on him to pay if he wishes to redeem himself from the hollowness, falsity, and self-deception (sweetly romantic though it may he) of that myth.

This metaphorical joining of one ghostly dream with another is established again through the image of the vanished, and now thoroughly (and safely) romanticized, Comanches. John Grady's father, another dying cowboy/rancher, tells him,

"We're like the Comanches was two hundred years ago" (25–26) in an attempt to soften the loss of the ranch, to evoke the presence of one "dream of the past" to join in mourning the passing of another, one equally "secular and transitory and violent" (5). But it is yet another memory of the past, which comes to John Grady as he sits at his dead grandfather's desk, that best signifies not only the persistent return of history through the liminal spaces of myth, but also the lesson John Grady must finally learn about the deceptive nature of the world seen through the blinders of national fantasy. As he sits in the darkened office, he can see through the window "[t]he black crosses of the old telegraph poles yoked across the constellations passing east to west. His grandfather said the Comanche would cut the wires and splice them back with horsehair" (11). In the illusion created by the splicing of what has been severed, McCarthy demonstrates the difficulty of seeing the world not as one would wish it to be, but as it actually is. While the wire may appear whole, it is nonetheless not functional. To paraphrase the Dueña Alfonsa, this is the difference between what is true and what is merely useful to believe, between the dream and the reality, myth and history. This is the world that lies waiting between the wish and the thing.

It is John Grady's naive and romantic inability to distinguish the truth—defined by the Dueña Alfonsa to be not "what is righteous but merely what is so"—which moves her to pay his and Rawlins's way out of prison but also, ultimately, causes her to reject his suit for Alejandra's hand (240). As she tells John Grady before she begins her tale, "You will see that those things which disposed me in your favor were the very things which led me to decide against you in the end" (231). Her entire monologue, the history of her life, is told for John Grady's benefit, and indeed, John Grady is a sort of male version of her young and idealistic self. Her journey may be seen as a tightly compressed parable of his. (...)

Despite the way in which many have read the novel, this is not a matter of juxtaposing innocent American romanticism with the brutal, violent realities of an inherently corrupt Mexico.[1]

American culpability in Mexican history and politics is clearly established in *Blood Meridian* and openly alluded to in *Pretty Horses*. I do not believe that McCarthy is attempting to posit America as the site of modernity and Mexico as simply a dream of the romanticized past, as Vereen Bell suggests, although John Grady may initially see it in just that way. Bell writes in "Between the Wish and the Thing the World Lies Waiting" that "John Grady and Rawlins escape for a time the dissociating effects of the technology and capital of the new American order, but what they get from their adopted ancient culture is an attractive but totalitarian hierarchy—the autocratic rule of families, at best, and at worst, of brute power instead of law. In Enlightenment terms, a dignified ancient culture is also, inescapably, a primitive one" (926). McCarthy has gone to great lengths, however, to point out that Mexican culture is no more "ancient" or "primitive" than American culture. Do the roots of Mexican culture stretch back to pre-Columbian indigenous peoples? John Grady rides through the ghosts of just such peoples on his own ranch and is watched by their living descendants upon his return to Texas. Is John Grady a nomad without a home in Mexico? He's still a homeless wanderer when he recrosses the border, and the brute power of law, explained to him by his father's attorney, has still robbed him of his patrimony. He is as helpless before its implacable and pitiless advance as he is before the corrupt captain in the Mexican jail. Neither can be cajoled, neither can be reasoned with, neither shows mercy or the slightest acknowledgment of John Grady's wishes, his code of honor, his view of how the world should be rather than how the world is.

In other words, the myth of the sacred cowboy, which demands that a worthy young man should end up with a ranch of his own, a lovely young wife, and "all the pretty horses" simply by virtue of being Anglo, male, a cowboy, and the descendant of colonizers, functions in neither world, and this is McCarthy's point. If we fall into the trap of believing that the code of the sacred cowboy was valid at some romanticized time in America's past, we will naturally assume that in an equally romanticized "old Mexico," where John Grady has symbolically traveled back in time, it will once again function properly. The world will be as the myth says it is. Reality, of course, proves the world to be far different. As Bell acknowledges, there is no escape possible, because "there is no human place outside of time, and where human places are there are also the constructs and institutional artifacts of history" (926).

This is as true, However, for the United States as it is for Mexico. It is not some ancient or primitive quality in Mexico that defeats John Grady; it is the hollowness and blindness of his faith—or, more properly, the hollowness of that myth upon which he has chosen to place his faith.[2] Like the peasants in Alfonsa's tale who desperately attempt to sell objects no one wants, John Grady clings to the values of a myth that hides the true nature of the world. He refuses or is unable to recognize that the falseness of the sacred cowboy is equivalent to the broken bits of machinery the peasants gather from the roads. The peasants' faith in a myth, in this case their belief in the value of all things associated with the industrialized world coupled with a profound ignorance of the true nature of that world, strengthens but also dooms them. The courage to see the world without ignorance and without faith, essentially without sentiments however attractive they may be, is what the Dueña Alfonsa wants John Grady to find through the story of her own life and the history of Mexico. (...)

John Grady struggles down the hard road to reach such a place himself through the final section of the novel. He begins to realize the hollowness of the myths into which he has poured his faith even before his long dialogue with Alfonsa, as he lies in the prison after the knife fight and feels a child's sorrow welling up inside him that "brought with it such pain that he stopped it cold and began at once his new life and the living of it breath to breath" (203). But while his new life, seen without the rosy filter of the mythic fantasy through which he has always viewed the world, might be said to begin here, his own place within that world is still unclear. No new mythic structure has emerged to replace the old one, and this is perhaps the most important part of the Dueña Alfonsa's lesson for John

Grady—that to distinguish what is true from what is useful to believe means to discard all the myths one's culture holds dear and make one's way in the world alone, with nothing but one's own courage to call upon, and all without ever falling into hopeless bitterness. This sort of existentialist epiphany, however, will never leave one unmarked, or even entirely whole. Such knowledge exacts a price, leaving one arguably reduced—like Gustavo with his glass eye and the Dueña with her missing fingers. (...)

Upon his return to Texas, John Grady is caught between two visions of the world, unable to return to the safe confines of the mythic past and as yet equally incapable of seeing how he must live his life in the future. He exists in a liminal space beyond myth, but not yet within history, a space within which "he felt wholly alien to the world although he loved it still" (282). His unfixed liminal status, betwixt and between myth and reality, truth and history, Mexico and the United States is figured by his physical appearance, like "some apparition out of the vanished past"—with his horses, guns, Mexican serape, and his inability to properly assess his relationship to the world to the point where he must ask what day it is, surprised to discover it is Thanksgiving (287). His quest to return Blevins's horse to its rightful owner is more properly a quest to release himself from the last hold of the myth of the sacred cowboy, signified in the national symbolic by the image of the horse. His confession to the judge does nothing to alleviate his pain, since what he receives from the judge is essentially the same lesson given to him by the Dueña Alfonsa: the task of fixing a way for himself in the world is one he must accomplish alone. (...)

In *Pretty Horses* McCarthy has manipulated the most familiar forms of national fantasy, icons constructing the most basic images commonly held in America of identity, nationality, and culture to make the coming-of-age of John Grady a story that speaks to the coming-of-age of a nation and causes the sorrowful and necessary death of a national fantasy. The ending here is ambiguous, not necessarily hopeful. As promised in the opening chapter, John Grady has redeemed himself in blood from the nostalgic blindness at the heart of the sacred cowboy myth, but whether this redemption is enough to carry him forward into the world to come remains obscured and unspoken at the close of this novel.

Notes

1. Tom Pilkington, for example, in "Fate and Free Will on the American Frontier" contrasts the United States to Mexico by calling the United States the "land of freedom" where "accountability and responsibility are the necessary complements of free will and volition" (321), while Dianne Luce sees Mexico as a "troubled Eden" (157), and Vereen Bell terms it "a totalitarian hierarchy," an "ancient culture," "a primitive one" (926) whose history is one of "horror and pathos" (924), and Daniel Cooper Alarcón argues that McCarthy has simply reproduced typical Anglo visions of Mexico as infernal paradise.

2. Cooper Alarcón suggests in *The Aztec Palimpsest* that John Grady is not defeated by Mexico, but rather, in a neocolonial extension of Manifest Destiny, triumphs by returning from the hell of the prison like a Campbell hero returning from the underworld. I would argue, however, that although John Grady survives, he enters Texas much reduced from the figure that rode boldly across the Rio Grande in the opening chapters, returning sans Blevins, Rawlins, money, and ranch—and with a broken heart to boot.

NANCY KREML ON STYLISTIC VARIATION AND COGNITIVE CONSTRAINT

The experience of reading *All the Pretty Horses* is often cinematic: we see details of setting and action clearly, but without overt interpretation, without description of inner states or even of possible ambiguous tones of voice or facial expression, without clearly stated evaluations, suggestions, judgments of characters and their actions. It is by manipulation of stylistic choice, in particular the interplay between two styles, that McCarthy is able, even so, to allow the reader access not only to the inner workings of the characters' minds but also to interpretations of the events of the novel. (...)

As the dominant style of the narrative voice, he establishes a transparent style, with little limitation of interpretation, against which he plays a secondary, more highly constrained foregrounded style; further, he uses the elements of the foregrounded style to signal a thematic shift, an intrusion of another level of meaning. Early in the novel, the foregrounded style occurs in fairly extended passages; as we learn to recognize its characteristics, he uses it more briefly and less often, so that a sentence of even a phrase evokes the significance of the style. This association of style and meaning becomes tine of the constraints on interpretation that guides us in recovering the implicatures of the text.

The transparent style is used for much of the novel, especially the narratives of action, as we see here in the account of John Grady and Rawlins as they wait for Blevins to retrieve his stolen horse:

> The boy slid from the horse and picked his way gingerly with his hare feet across the mad to the horse and looked in. Then he climbed through the window.
> What the hell's he doin? said Rawlins.
> You got me.
> They waited. He didnt come back.
> Yonder comes somebody.
> Some dogs started up. John Grady mounted up and turned the horse and went back up the road and sat the horse in the dark. Rawlins followed. Dogs were beginning to bark all back through the town. A light came on.
> This is by God it, aint it? said Rawlins.
> John Grady looked at him. He was sitting with life carbine upright on his thigh. From beyond the buildings and the din of dogs there came a shout.
> You know what these sons of bitches'll do to us? said Rawlins. You thought about that?
> John Grady leaned forward and spoke to the horse and put his hand on the horse's shoulder. The horse had begun to step nervously and it was not a nervous horse. He looked toward the houses where they'd seen the light.

A horse whinnied in the dark.

That crazy son of a bitch, said Rawlins. That crazy son of a bitch (82–83).

This style seems to be the plainest possible in English. The syntax is basic: sentences are almost invariably ordered subject-verb-(complement): "the boy slid," "Rawlins pulled," "they rode," and so on. In the transparent style, verbs and their arguments stand unmodified, in clear and strong relation to each other; rarely do introductory or intervening phrases interfere with the clear statement of action. The directness and immediacy of the syntax embodies that of the scene. We find few adjectives, either as preceders of nouns or as complements, and few adverbs formed from adjectives. Most of the adverbial information concerns time and place, rarely manner: "across the road," "in the dark." Both nouns and verbs are usually concrete, morphologically simple, and of Anglo-Saxon derivation: "slice," "rode," "shoal," "high," etc. The rhythm of these monosyllables, like beating hooves, is often strong and regular. (...)

This is the standard style, the unmarked norm, of the novel. Remarkably, it is used for the most crucial scenes:[1] we find it not only in scenes of getting dressed and feeding horses, buying food and closing gates, but in scenes central to the plot: the descriptions of the mother's stage performance (21–22), the execution of Blevins (177–78), the prison Murder (199–202), the last meeting of John Grady and Alejandra (247–48), among others. In these passages the language appears limited, precise, but powerful; the style honors the action. (...)

Such undirected interpretation is not found in another style of the narrative voice, the opaque, which is shown all the more opaque by its contrast with the transparent.[4] Because the transparent style is so transparent, so unforegrounded, the appearance of the opaque style suddenly draws the reader's attention to the language and to the significance of McCarthy's stylistic choices. We first learn to recognize its characteristics in extended passages like the remainder of the paragraph describing the departure for Mexico:

> They rode out on the high prairie where they slowed the horses to a walk and the stars swarmed around them out of the blackness. They heard somewhere in that tenant-less night a bell that tolled and ceased where no bell was and they rode out on the round dais of the earth which alone was dark and no light to it and which carried their figures and bore them up into the swarming stars so that they rode not under but among them and they rode at once jaunty and circumspect, like thieves newly loosed in that dark electric, like young thieves in a glowing orchard, loosely jacketed against the cold and ten thousand worlds for the choosing (30).

The introduction of metaphor—"stars swarmed"—marks the transition of the riders from the town to the high prairie (the beginning of their journey) and stylistically marks the introduction of the opaque style. Now we find subordination: "where no bell was," "so that they rode," "like thieves newly loosed"; and modification: "that tenantless night," "the swarming stars," "young thieves in a glowing orchard." (...)

The shift to the opaque style in such a sustained passage clearly functions to focus our attention on the language itself. Such passages occur at several points where the action of the novel suddenly shifted to another plane, where the presence of some powerful force is felt—not always evil. The novel opens with the most sustained of such passages—almost all of the first five pages are in this style, including John Grady's sight of his grandfather in the casket (3), the howling trails (3–4), the vision of the Indian ghosts (5–6); later, such passages presage the loss and recovery of Blevins' horse (73) and the arrival at La Purísima (93); they describe the horses (105, 128) and John Grady's lovemaking with Alejandra (141); they are used for his dreams of horses while in prison (161) and while transporting the captured captain (280), the death of the doe (282), and the final passage where he rides away, still leading Blevins' horse (302). The use of the style in matter: if not with portents of evil or dreams of lost innocence, at least with the sudden realization of the greater dimensions of actions. In these passages, McCarthy constrains us to see the meaning of the events; we are not at liberty to take them as simple actions. But the passages also teach us their language; we learn to associate it with this kind of meaning so that we do not need a sustained passage to evoke the sense of foreboding evil or transcendent joy. A sentence, a phrase or even a word can be so clearly marked with this style that we recognize the sign, just as even one word of Spanish comes to summon up the culture of the speaker. (...)

Thus it is the interaction of styles in this novel that allows us access to the inner workings of characters' minds, and even more, to the workings of the narrative. The transparent style shows us the action of the novel, but action whose causes and consequences are unclear; the opaque suggests the framework for recognizing the meaning of these actions. By investing that style itself with the significance of constraint, the author is able to control our reading of the text without violating its apparent cinematic distance.

Notes

1. Growing out of early Speech Act Theory, as developed by Austin and Searle, and out of the concept of implicature developed by Grice, a recent theory of cognition and communication, Relevance Theory, has been developed by Sperber and Wilson to account for the process by which implied communication is appropriately understood. Writers must use "acts of ostension" or noticeable signals to draw the readers' attention to the fact that art implicature is being made, which derives its meaning from something in the "shared cognitive environment," and must assume that readers will select the most obvious or most easily seen aspect of that context as the implied message.

4. Many readers consider the opaque style to be the "poetic," because of its literary lexicon and syntax, and yet, as we have seen, the transparent style has many of those qualities often associated with poetry—concreteness, economy, suggestiveness. For that reason the distinction made here is between "transparent" and "opaque" rather than between "poetic" and "prosaic."

Dianne C. Luce on John Grady Cole's Heroism

What has McCarthy given us here—American fiction's "last action hero"?

It is quite possible that John Grady initially sees himself so. The novel is suffused with evidence of his immaturity, his romanticism, his grandiosity, his disappointed sense of entitlement. John Grady's childish vision of himself as romantic hero is, however, repeatedly challenged and ultimately modified by his experience. Alfonsa's commentary on the fate of the Maderos aptly describes the direction of McCarthy's plot: "The world is quite ruthless in selecting between the dream and the reality, even where we will not. Between the wish and the thing the world lies waiting" (238). John Grady is not the static hero of the adventure novel who triumphs unchanged and unscarred by his ordeals. Rather, he is the romantic dreamer who gradually awakens to reality, which always lies waiting to test him, and who responds by abandoning his quest for dominance and courageously embracing instead a quest for truth and understanding. This is his true heroism. (...)

One of the ways in which McCarthy undercuts John Grady's romantic heroism is by showing that his young protagonist confuses the ardor of his desire with his right to attain its object. He has been raised to feel that his right and proper place in the world is on his family's ranch: as his grandfather's sole male heir, he is entitled to it genetically and by the right of primogeniture that had given the land entire to his grandfather and appears to have fated the seven younger brothers to die early and violently.[3] When John Grady loses the ranch through his grandfather's death and his parent's divorce, he sets out to regain this lost paradise[4] in another country.

At the point of his departure, McCarthy deftly emphasizes both John Grady's romantic view of his adventure and the reality that underlies it:

[T]hey rode out on the round dais of the earth ... which carried their figures and bore them into the swarming stars so that they rode not under but among them and they rode at once jaunty and circumspect, like thieves newly loosed in that dark electric, like young thieves in a glowing orchard, loosely jacketed against the cold and ten thousand worlds for the choosing (30).

The harshest view one may take of John Grady's ambition is that it is congruent with the American frontier tradition of the land grab. He and Rawlins and Blevins cross into Mexico "like a party of marauders" (45), and indeed this is how Don Héctor comes to view them with some reason. Idealist that he is, John Grady would not consciously undertake such an enterprise, but Rawlins sees fairly clearly his complicated motives for culti-vating Don Héctor and the dueña Alfonsa. When John Grady confesses that he has eyes for Alejandra, Rawlins bluntly asks, "You got eyes for the spread?" (138). Earlier, when Rawlins commented that there was a lot of country in Mexico to be searched for "that paradise," John Grady admitted, "That's what I'm here for" (59). Although in 1949 John Grady cannot acquire land, not even in Mexico, in the way his great-grandfa-ther had, his father has shown him that if one can neither claim nor inherit land, he can marry it. (...)

Alfonsa is less interested in control than in responsible choices, and she does not insist on her right to say until John Grady demonstrates that he does not understand her warning about consequences to Alejandra if her reputation were to be com-promised. He attempts to dismiss the aspects of reality that do not match his idea of what seems right.

> Right? she said. Oh. Yes. Well.
> She turned one hand in the air as if reminded of some-thing she'd misplaced. No, she said. No. It's not a matter of right. You must understand. It is a matter of who must say (137).

She is reminded that with John Grady she is speaking to a child, and one of an alien culture to boot: alien despite his fluent Spanish and his experience with his family's Mexican-American workers, despite even his love for the *abuela*. John Grady wants to be the one who must say. He has yet to outgrow the grandiosity and self-centeredness of childhood, and his journey into Mexico is an exercise in self-will.

Rocked in his saddle, this dreaming infant has ventured into an alien land, stirring restlessly but dreaming on when the candilleros offer to buy Jimmy Blevins; when Rawlins warns him that Blevins is a loose cannon; when the Mexicans at La Encantada impound the Blevins horse, demonstrating their conception of "right"; when Don Héctor communicates the official Mexican view of the Americans who have stolen back the Blevins horse; when Alfonsa charges him actively to protect Alejandra's reputation.[7] It takes three closely fired shots—his and Rawlins' arrest, the revelation that Blevins has killed a man, and the murder of Blevins—to begin to wake him, to break the enchantment. As John Grady makes choices, the world lies waiting to confront him with their consequences. His growth in heroism is partially structured around these choices or tests, partially around his rejection or acceptance of a series of mentors and models, chief among which are Rawlins, Alfonsa, and the judge; and Blevins and the Encantada caption as negative models.

Though more secularized, the issue of judgment is as central to *All the Pretty Horses* as to *Blood Meridian* and *Outer Dark*. All of John Grady's troubles derive from errors in judgment or, worse, his refusal to make conscious choices instead of sleepwalking through Mexico.[8] The consequences of his actions together with other's assessments of him (John Grady is questioned and judged by at least six different persons who determine his right to attain various of his wishes: his employer Don Héctor, Alejandra's dueña, Alfonsa, the unjust captain at la Encantada, Pérez in the prison at Saltillo, Alejandra both when she accepts him as her lover and when she refuses to marry him, and the Texas judge who awards him Blevins' horse) gradually teach him to honor reality over fantasy, truth over expediency, courage over avoidance; and because he is willing to endure necessary physical and emotional pain in a series of ordeals imposed on him by the world of reality, he returns from Mexico with his integrity restored.[9]

Many of the trials John Grady endures derive from Jimmy Blevins, that human lightning rod who appears on the scene almost the moment John Grady and Rawlins set off for Mexico and almost as mysteriously as Judge Holden appeared to Glanton's gang, out of nowhere, on a rock in the middle of the desert in *Blood Meridian*. As much as Alejandra, Jimmy represents temptation, and like Judge Holden—though he appears more innocent and proves pitiably killable—Jimmy functions on one level as a principle of evil. He has much in common with that less ambiguous avatar of evil, the Encantada captain, who comes to the novel's fore as Jimmy is about to be eliminated: neither will stand to be laughed at;[10] both feel somehow entitled to the magnificent horse and justified in killing; both are practitioners of egocentric rationalization and, like the kid early in *Blood Meridian* (3), devotees of mindless violence.

Rawlins rightly distrusts Jimmy immediately but lacks, as always, the courage of his convictions to insist that John Grady listen. Blevins is clearly a runaway, probably a horsethief, and more practiced with a gun than any thirteen-year-old should be. His assertion that the older boys should allow him to ride with them because he is an American (45) is an ominous echo of the ethnocentrism and racism at the heart of *Blood Meridian*'s violence, a sly insinuation that he is "one of us" and that Mexicans are "other," and indeed a reflection of John Grady's unacknowledged opportunism. It is nearly impossible to insult Blevins except by laughing at him, but he tells the boys he would have killed his stepfather before taking a beating (64) and he would have killed Rawlins if his joke about murdering him had been in earnest (49). In neither instance is he hotheaded, but rather coolly self-possessed; and when he ultimately recovers his gun from the man in La Encantada, shooting him because he "come at me" and excusing himself by asking "What choice did I have?" (159–60),[11] we can hardly be surprised. Jimmy is self-serving violence masquerading as childish innocence, or, more chilling still—conjoined with it.

John Grady is easily taken in. He identities with Jimmy's plight and reflexively defends him against Rawlins' carping. The candilleros' attempt to buy Jimmy places him squarely in the pawn's role and commits John Grady further to acting the knight (a role John Grady invariably finds seductive but in which he is often as misguided and destructive as Don Quixote, to whom Don Héctor compares him [146]). John Grady's motto, "No such thing as a mean colt" (103), serves him better in the horse-breaking venture than it does in his dealings with Blevins. By the time he encounters the young cuchillero at Saltillo, in whose eyes he reads a "malign history burning cold and remote and black" (200), he has abandoned such sentiments. But before Jimmy proves himself a ready assassin, John Grady sees him as "just a kid" (56) and fails to recognize the potential for meanness behind his youthful and ludicrous facade. (...)

As John Grady leaves his friend Rawlins in San Angelo, this boy who wanted so desperately to find a permanent homestead is clearly setting forth for a future of wandering in "the world to come" (302). Rawlins asks him, "Where is your country?" and John Grady sadly answers, "I dont know where it is. I dont know what happens to country" (299). Gail Morrison has suggested that pragmatically at least John Grady's possession of the Blevins horse and his knowledge of horse breeding are the basis for a potentially solid future (178, 183). But I find the novel's resolution less optimistic. John Grady's journey, like those of so many of McCarthy's protagonists, is an initiation into evil. He has rejected his boy's fantasy of the world as potentially an Eden, and he knows now that he inhabits a mysteriously fallen world and is part of it. (...)

Ultimately John Grady earns our respect as "hero" rather than mere protagonist because of his acceptance of what Alfonsa so generously tells him: that in courageously acting on what is true, he has "nothing to lose" (239).[15]

Notes

3. In one sense, the history of John Grady's family suggests that his real heritage is death before the age of twenty-five unless he inherits the land. At the end of the novel, he agrees with the judge that he will get it sorted out "If I live" (293)—a suggestion that he has internalized the lessons of his family history as well as those learned in Mexico.

John Grady's anger at his disinheritance is especially clear when he argues that Rawlins should join him in his journey into Mexico: "What the hell reason you got for stayin? You think somebody's goin to die and leave you somethin?" (27).

4. For a discussion of the edenic themes in the novel, see Gail Moore Morrison's "*All the Pretty Horses*: John Grady's Expulsion from Paradise."

7. If Alfonsa's charge to John Grady is seen as a kind of heroic task to be performed in order to win the hand of his lady, his failure is clear.

8. At what Rawlins correctly perceives to be a point of no return, he tries to convince John Grady of the wisdom of leaving Blevins outside of La Encantada instead of helping him recover his horse: "Ever dumb thing I ever done in my life there was a decision I made before that got me into it. It was never the dumb thing. It was always some choice I'd made before it" (79).

9. Obviously, I disagree with Vereen Bell's assertion that the point of the novel is "whether John Grady can endure such gratuitous tribulation with his hardheaded boy's idealism intact" (921). His idealism misleads him sometimes so seriously as to compromise his integrity. I think the point of the novel is more whether John Grady can understand and accept the consequences of his own choices, as well as gratuitous tribulation, without despairing, without abandoning himself and thus breaking faith with others.

10. When Jimmy falls backward off the bench at the Mexican family's dinner table, he slinks away, saying, "I dont like to be laughed at" (53). The captain, more deeply ripened in ruthlessness, alludes to his violent treatment of a whore when he was a youngster. He suspected that the older boys had paid her to refuse him, "So they can laugh ... But I dont let whores make trouble for me" he says. "When I come back there is no laughing. No one is laughing. You see. That has always been my way in this world. I am the one when I go someplace then there is no laughing. When I go there then they slop laughing" (181).

11. Blevins' excuse is one of several instances in which characters claim that their actions were determined by lack of choice. Consider, for example, the Texas judge's story about his decision to accept the

responsibility of sitting in judgment on others: "I just saw a lot of injustice in the court system and I saw people my own age in positions of authority that I had grown up with and knew for a calcified fact didn't have one damn lick of sense. I think I just didnt have any choice. Just didn't have any choice" (292). Though the judge echoes Jimmy, his is a decision that accepts the adult responsibility to make hard choices in an uncertain world. Perhaps less justifiably, John Grady decides to help Blevins recover his horse despite Rawlins' warnings: "He looked at Rawlins rolled asleep in his soogan and he knew that he was right in all he'd said and there was no help for it" (81). And Rawlins responds to John Grady's conclusion that the Encantada captain wants to make a deal so that they will keep quiet about Blevins with the comment, "Like we had some kind of a choice" (179). Though such statements in McCarthy's work frequently—and certain in Jimmy's case—raise the possibility of self-delusion, of too readily abandoning the responsibility of conscious choice, it is hard not to agree with Rawlins' conclusion that when John Grady killed the cuchillero he "didnt have no choice" (215). In this instance, John Grady recognizes that he must defend himself from the assassin, makes deliberate preparations to do so, saves his own life by killing the cuchillero who assaults him, but then in a spontaneous revulsion of feeling repudiates his act, casting the knife away from his (201). At the end of the novel he is still struggling to accommodate this necessary choice to act for his own life in preference to his assassin's, and the judge's compassion for John Grady's struggle and his modeling the mature acceptance of responsibility for life and death decisions are potentially healing.

15. As perceptive as he often is, Rawlins does not achieve heroic stature because he is not true to himself: he allows his fear to overcome his regard for truth. His very presence in Mexico is a kind of lie, since his heart is never in the adventure. His willingness to accept the captain's lies when he is tortured is a degradation in which John Grady does not share. Rawlins is finally more true to himself when he leaves John Grady and returns home, but this act involves his acquiescing in the lie that has given the Mexicans at La Encantada possession of his horse. As Rawlins very well understands, John Grady risks Blevins' fate when he returns to La Encantada for the three horses. Rawlins is not willing to risk; John Grady is. And as John Grady tells Rawlins, "I aint Blevins" (213).

In Cormac McCarthy's *All the Pretty Horses,* after John Grady Cole survives the prison in Saltillo and returns to the Hacienda de Nuestra Señora de la Purísima Concepcion. Dueña Alfonsa takes the time to tell him her life's story "because among other reasons" she thinks "we should know who our enemies are" (241). Her story explains much more though. She gives a detailed account of Francisco and Gustavo Madero, two American and European educated brothers her brother had mentioned earlier to Cole. Don Hector dismissed the Maderos and "these ideas" they learned in Europe with a flippant wave claiming that they would never work because "One country is not another country. Mexico is not Europe" (145). Dueña Alfonsa does not dismiss these two men so lightly. In telling Cole, and ostensibly us, about these two men, Alfonsa discusses two men who held power for only fifteen months (November 1911-February 1913) and whose presidency failed to bring about the social changes Francisco envisioned. Her narrative contrasts that of historians who tend to focus on General Victoriana Huerta, the man who overthrew Madero and had him and his brother assassinated; General Reves, a revolutionary whose threatened conspiracy kept the Maderos occupied; and the famous folk hero Francisco "Pancho" Villa. In doing so, she relegates the men who actually gained and sustained power to secondary status and subverts the normal hierarchical status by privileging the loser. By telling Cole about a failed president, she explains what did not happen in Mexico. The implications of her story reach beyond revisionist history. Her narrative contends that the "absent" history, what did not happen, has as great an effect as the history that did not occur. (...)

The information Dueña Alfonsa tells John Grady Cole about Franscisco Madero is historically accurate. In effect, her narrative is just as much Madero's history as are "standard" histories of him, such as Stanley R. Ross's *Francis Madero: Apostle of Mexican Democracy*, Alan Knight's *The Mexican Revolution*, and Gene Z. Hanrahan's *Counter Revolution Along the Border*. Dueña

Alfonsa's story reinforces the archived history's perspective. She tells Cole that Francisco set "up schools for the poor ... dispensed medicines ... [and fed] hundreds of people from his own kitchen"(233).[1] Her dates, places, and names of acquaintances are accurate, as well. Her narrative about him, though, incorporates much more into the novel. By introducing his name into the story, she creates a climate in which Madero's cultural influence becomes relevant. Our knowledge of mainstream history informs our read of her "fictional" history, and both inform her interpretation of the novel. Once Madero's name has entered the discourse of the novel, his personal history reacts intertextually with the narrative. To begin to understand the text, we need to know what images the Madero name creates according to Ross, et al. and the authorized histories. Only then can we begin to comprehend the full implications of the history Dueña Alfonsa relates as fiction but can be drawn as real. (...)

The implications of Dueña Alfonsa's story to John Grady Cole extend much farther than simply a history lesson, though. The facts of her story reflect the standard bias of history, but her history refocuses our attention on what has not taken place in Mexico because of Madero's failed presidency. The working class lost power and was once again relegated to second-class citizenship. In essence, her narrative is as much a prescription as a description. It is not simply that she revises history, she refocuses history. Historians have treated Francisco much like Don Héctor does; they flippantly wave him aside, assuming that his ideas "were quite radical" (144). Dueña Alfonsa refuses to accept that explanation, and her story creates a new history of Franscisco that demonstrates that these radical ideas were in the best interest of the majority of Mexico.

When Cole and Rawlins prepare to leave Texas and cross the border, neither Madero nor Mexican history is part of their consciousness. When they look at a map of the region, they look at a map that has "roads and rivers and towns on the American side of the map as far South as the Rio Grande and beyond that all was white," and Rawlins exclaims that "There aint shit down there" (34). Alan Cheuse posits that Cole seeks "freedom from the old well-marked Texas spaces in the possibilities of an undiscovered country" and that a mapped territory "means having a past, both personal and historical" (141). Cheuse's interpretation raises some interesting questions. If Cheuse is correct, then Cole and Rawlins are searching for a new identity in a place that has no identity. This implies that people living in this uncharted territory have no past; and, thus, since they have no basis to explain their existence, no history for them equals no power.[12] Alfonsa wants to give these people a new history, Madero as the leader of the common man. If she can provide his story, she can create their story. The narrative of the text reinforces her story by continually showing how Madero did [not] affect Mexico.

The narrative explicitly mentions the existing poverty in its descriptions of the houses and/or appearances of the natives. At Cole, Rawlins, and Blevins's first stop, they ride into Reforma, a town of "Half a dozen low houses with walls of mud brick slumping into ruins" (49). (The town's name, although real, is ironic in light of what has not occurred in Mexico.) This is a town where "There aint no electricity" (51). A girl, comic book reading age, works the bar, and her parents, if they are even alive, they do not make an appearance. As the boys ride on, they stop for the night at an *astancia* where the family feeds them and offers shelter. The man refuses payment for the food, and his actions speak of nobility and a comfortable existence. But the narrative subverts this read. The family generously offers food, yet this testifies to their goodness and nobility more so than to their financial situation. Theirs is a family still scratching and clawing to live in a mud house with no electricity and "with old calendars and magazine pictures" as decoration. More importantly, though, when Cole asks him about "work in this part of the country," the man sends them "yon side of the Sierra de Carmen. About three hundred kilometers. He made that country sound like the Big Rock Candy Mountains" (55). The reference to the Big Rock Candy Mountains could be a reminder of the age of these two young men. Rawlins examination of his wallet, and the hole in Betty Ward's "schooldays picture" reminds us that these are two teenage boys who have not yet seen enough of life to know how harsh it can be."[13] Arguably though, the reference to a mythical land farther south reinforces the possibility that the land this man sends them to does not exist. He sends them south so that they can ply their trade.[14] This farmer sends him to a mythical place with "lakes and runnin water and grass to the stirrups" (55). If Madero's reforms had worked, perhaps this place might exist. And paradoxically, if Madero had succeeded, the farmer would not have to send Cole searching farther south for work.[15] (...)

John Grady Cole's experiences supplement and authorize Dueña Alfonsa's story. She gives Cole, and the reader, the history of the loser. Madero lost and the people of Mexico lost. By losing power, they lost control of the flow of information. They could not tell their story. Dueña Alfonsa does and gives a capable, intelligent history of Francisco Madero. Cole's encounters and experiences invigorate her narrative because we see, in the Mexican characters, the effects of Madero's failure. *All the Pretty Horses* works not just as a fictional novel, but as a history of twentieth-century Mexican politics. In the final analysis, then, the novel, through Dueña Alfonsa, questions the accuracy of "archived" history. Dueña Alfonsa's narrative may parallel what historians will later authorize as the truth, but her story also adds to that truth. The resultant fiction she creates as history becomes validated by the experiences of John Grady Cole.

Notes

1. This quote by Shelby Foote is on the back cover of Sepich's book and is predictable praise from a historian, but we should not dismiss it because of that. Sepich might show us how McCarthy "built" the text, but it is up to us to uncover why he built it the way he did.

12. In many ways I am relying on Gerda Lerner's idea in *Creation of Patriarchy*. She argues that people with no history lack power because they have no base or history to draw from. If they have no history, they have no stories or myths that give them direction and truth to

follow. Although her study discusses women and gender issues, her thesis is germane to this topic as well.

13. At this stage of the journey, John Grady and Rawlins probably do still believe in the Big Rock Candy Mountain. Later in the novel, Cole meets a proprietor of a café who tells him "that it was good that God kept the truths of life from the young as they were starting out or else they'd have no heart to start at all" (286). Cole and Rawlins do not know the truths they will encounter shortly. If so, they would know that traveling 300 kilometers would not place them at the Big Rock Candy Mountain.

14. In one way, Cole left Texas because he lost his ability to sell his "labour-power" (Marx 186). When Cole's mother refuses to let him run the ranch, she takes his ability to sell his commodity from him. Arguably, this novel is his search for a place to offer his "Labour-power" for sale. In many ways Madero's goal was to create a country that allowed for that possibility. What exists in Mexico is vastly different. Marx envisioned a system where "buyer" and "seller" were both equal in the eyes of the law (186). We can pick any worker-owner situation in the novel and see that equality does not exist.

15. Cole's reference to Big Rock Candy Mountain calls forth more than one significant Wallace Stegner's novel, the song, and the child's idea to name a few. Each of these informs the rhetoric of the text, and each one helps shape our interpretation. Stegner's novel seems particularly appropriate considering the protagonist continually searches for life on easy street. This reference works as a subtle foreshadowing to what Cole will not find as he travels farther south.

Works by Cormac McCarthy

The Orchard Keeper, 1965.

Outer Dark, 1968.

Child of God, 1973.

The Gardener's Son (teleplay for PBS), 1977.

Suttree, 1979.

Blood Meridian, or the Evening Redness in the West, 1985.

All the Pretty Horses, 1992.

The Stonemason, 1994.

The Crossing, 1994.

Cities of the Plain, 1998.

Annotated Bibliography

Alarcón, Daniel Cooper. "All The Pretty Mexicos: Cormac McCarthy's Mexican Representations." *Cormac McCarthy: New Directions.* Ed. James D. Lilley. Albuquerque: University of New Mexico Press, 2002: pp. 141–149.

Alarcón argues that All The Pretty Horses fits into the model of the "Infernal Paradise," in which the Mexican setting represents a symbolic backdrop for the enchanted American hero. Thus, McCarthy's Mexico is a romantic, nostalgic landscape, and the novel fails to challenge these ideals.

Arnold, Edwin T. "'Go to Sleep': Dreams and Visions in the Border Trilogy." *A Cormac McCarthy Companion: The Border Trilogy.* Ed. Edwin T. Arnold and Dianne C. Luce. Jackson: University Press of Mississippi, 2001: pp. 37–72.

Analyzes roles of dreams and visions in the Border Trilogy, and how the devices provide insights into characters and their experiences.

Arnold, Edwin T. and Dianne C. Luce. "Introduction." *Perspectives on Cormac McCarthy.* Jackson: University Press of Mississippi, 1999.

Provides bibliographical information on McCarthy, and examines the rise in scholarly attention of his work.

Bell, Vereen M. *The Achievement of Cormac McCarthy.* Baton Rouge: Louisiana State University Press, 1988.

Published before *All the Pretty Horses*, this book examines the "prevailing gothic and nihilistic mood" of McCarthy's first four novels. Groundbreaking for being the first published book-length study of McCarthy's work.

Busby, Mark. "Into the Darkening Land, the World to Come: Cormac McCarthy's *Border Crossings*." *Myth, Legend, Dust:*

Critical Responses to Cormac McCarthy. Ed. Rick Wallach. New York: Manchester University Press, 2000. pp. 227–48.

Focuses on the repeating metaphor of border crossings in the *Border Trilogy*. Busby shows how the border is complicated and ambiguous, a fusion of frontier and civilization. Examines themes of illusion/reality and individual/community. Busby argues that as John Grady's journey progresses, his knowledge of the world expands.

Cheuse, Alan. "A Note on Landscape in *All The Pretty Horses*." *Southern Quarterly* 30, (Summer 1992): pp. 140–42.

This brief essay asserts that McCarthy's setting does not function as merely background, but is a living part of the novel, with multiple meanings and forms.

Holloway, David. *The Late Modernism of Cormac McCarthy*. Westport, CT: Greenwood Press, 2002.

Examines the unconscious ideological assumptions of the work and the positions of other critics. Defines McCarthy as neither a postmodernist nor a modernist, but as a "late modernist." In other words, the novels are characteristic of their historical moment; yet also assume a subversive posture toward the qualities that define that moment.

Guillemin, George. "As of Some Site Where Life Had Not Succeeded." *Southern Quarterly* 38, no. 3 (Spring 2000): 72–98. Rpt. *A Cormac McCarthy Companion: The Border Trilogy*. Ed. Edwin T. Arnold and Dianne C. Luce. Jackson: UP of Mississippi: 2001. 92–130.

Analyzes The *Border Trilogy*'s stylistic, structural, and semantic complexity, and demonstrates how allegory and melancholia combine to redefine pastoralism.

Jarrett, Robert L. *Cormac McCarthy*. New York: Twayne Publishers, 1997.

Examines and analyzes all of McCarthy's books to date. In chapter five, "*The Border Trilogy*: Individualism, History, and

Cultural Crossings," Jarrett analyzes The *Border Trilogy* as postmodern fiction. *All The Pretty Horses*, he asserts, both imitates and critiques the Western. Jarrett also discusses themes and the various quests, such as the quest for identity and its limits.

Kreml, Nancy. "Stylistic Variation and Cognitive Constraint in *All The Pretty Horses.*" *Sacred Violence: A Reader's Companion to Cormac McCarthy.* Ed. Wade Hall and Rick Wallach. El Paso: Texas Western Press, 1995. pp. 137–48.

Examines two styles of the narrative voice, what Kreml terms the transparent style and the opaque style. Demonstrates how the interaction of theses two styles allows the reader access to the characters' minds and to the workings of the narrative. Kreml closely analyzes McCarthy's use of syntax, word choices, and prose rhythms, in showing how the language affects the narrative.

Lilley, James D. " 'The Hands of Yet Other Puppets' : Figuring Freedom and Reading Repetition in *All The Pretty Horses.*" *Myth, Legend, Dust: Critical Responses to Cormac McCarthy.* Ed. Rick Wallach. New York: Manchester University Press, 2000. pp. 272–287.

Discusses themes of fate in McCarthy's novel, analyzing the use of repetition and language. The article focuses on John Grady and the Dueña Alfonsa, and the push and pull of their interaction. This essay refers to theories of Lacan, and examines language and its limits among the characters, as well as the themes of control and power.

Luce, Dianne C. "'When You Wake': John Grady Cole's Heroism in *All The Pretty Horses.*" *Sacred Violence: A Reader's Companion to Cormac McCarthy.* Ed. Wade Hall and Rick Wallach. El Paso: Texas Western Press, 1995. pp. 155–167.

Luce provides examples and analysis of John Grady's journey from a romantic dreamer to a hero who faces reality with courage. This article argues against notions of Grady as a standard, static hero of the adventure novel, and portrays him as a complex and evolving hero.

Morrison, Gail Moore. *"All The Pretty Horses:* John Grady Cole's Expulsion from Paradise" *Perspectives on Cormac McCarthy.* Ed. Edwin T. Arnold and Dianne C. Luce. Jackson: University Press of Mississippi, 1999: pp. 175–194.

Analyzes the sophisticated structure of the novel, focusing John Grady Cole's physical and metaphysical odyssey. Morrison emphasizes the novel as a coming-of-age story, following John Grady Cole's journey to and from Mexico, and focuses on the allegorical, and Biblical symbolism of the novel, charting Grady's fall from Paradise.

Owens, Barcley. *Cormac McCarthy's Western Novels.* Tucson: The University of Arizona Press, 2000.

Focuses on *Blood Meridian* and *The Border Trilogy*. In chapter four, "Western Myths in *All The Pretty Horses* and *The Crossing*" Owens posits that these two novels follow a traditional Western prototype and that the protagonists are traditional "Adam-American" heroes. Arguing that *All The Pretty Horses* follows a classic Western structure, Owens believes the novel to be a significant departure from McCarthy's violent and ambitious *Blood Meridian*.

Pilkington, Tom. "Fate and Free Will on the American Frontier: Cormac McCarthy's Western Fiction." *Western American Literature* 27 (Winter 1993): pp. 311–22.

Examines how John Grady's beliefs in freedom, free will, and individualism, lead him to a code to live by, of "honor and responsibility."

Shaw, Patrick. "Female Presence, Male Violence, and the Art of Artlessness in *The Border Trilogy*." *Southwestern American Literature* 25, no. 1, 1999: pp. 11–23.

Examines motifs of feminine presence and masculine violence in *All The Pretty Horses* and *The Crossing*, and interprets repeating metaphors and themes.

Snyder, Phillip A. "Cowboy Codes in Cormac McCarthy's Border Trilogy." *A Cormac McCarthy Companion: The Border Trilogy*. Ed. Edwin T. Arnold and Dianne C. Luce. Jackson: University Press of Mississippi, 2001: pp. 198–227.

Snyder defines the binary figures of what he terms McCarthy's "cowboy codes." He argues that cowboy culture does not operate in "unified totality" but as "infinite heterogeneity." By using these figures, Snyder analyzes how *The Border Trilogy* follows the shifts and displacements of the American cowboy identity. Snyder suggests that McCarthy reaffirms, while also critiques and renovates, traditional cowboy codes.

Spurgeon, Sara L. "'Pledged in Blood': Truth and Redemption in Cormac McCarthy's *All The Pretty Horses*." *Western American Literature* 34, no. 1 (Spring 1999): pp. 25–44.

Examines the myths of the cowboy in Western culture, and argues that McCarthy subverts these myths: "McCarthy lovingly evokes that myth and at the same time strips away the layers of fantasy that make belief in it possible." Spurgeon provides a strong character analysis of Alfonsa and John Grady, arguing that it is Grady's "blindness of faith" that threatens to defeat him. This essay also examines the role that economic class plays in the novel.

Sullivan, Nell. "Boys Will Be Boys And Girls Will Be Gone." *A Cormac McCarthy Companion: The Border Trilogy*. Ed. Edwin T. Arnold and Dianne C. Luce. Jackson: UP of Mississippi, 2001. pp. 228–255.

Examines how gender roles, as defined in the context of a Western narrative, are destabilized in *The Border Trilogy*. Sullivan argues although women are eliminated or contained in the novels, the feminine remains and is "performed" by male characters. Examines male-to-male desires and the subversion of gender roles.

Wegner, John. "Whose Story is It? History and Fiction in Cormac McCarthy's *All The Pretty Horses.*" *The Southern Quarterly 36* no. 2. (Winter 1998): pp. 103–110.

Focuses on the Dueña Alfonsa narrating both her life story and the history of Mexico. Wegner explains that by telling the story of the Madero brothers, Alfonsa evokes a part of Mexico's history that is often left out: "The implications of her story reach beyond revisionist history. Her narrative contends that the "absent" history, what did not happen, has as great an effect as the history that did occur."

Woodson, Linda Townley. "Deceiving the Will to Truth: The Semiotic Foundation of *All The Pretty Horses.*" *Sacred Violence: A Reader's Companion to Cormac McCarthy.* Ed. Wade Hall and Rick Wallach. El Paso: Texas Western Press, 1995: pp. 149–154.

This article claims that Michael Foucault's theory of "the will to truth," a distrust of the language that represents desire and power, forms the semiotic foundation for *All The Pretty Horses.* Townley traces the many "lessons" John Grady is given to try to make him understand the truth, and shows what he has learned from both these lessons and his own experiences.

Woodward, Richard B. "Cormac McCarthy's Venomous Fiction." *New York Times Magazine* (April 19, 1992): pp. 28–31+. McCarthy's only published interview to date.

Contributors

Harold Bloom is Sterling Professor of the Humanities at Yale University and Henry W. and Albert A. Berg Professor of English at the New York University Graduate School. He is the author of over 20 books, including *Shelley's Mythmaking* (1959), *The Visionary Company* (1961), *Blake's Apocalypse* (1963), *Yeats* (1970), *A Map of Misreading* (1975), *Kabbalah and Criticism* (1975), *Agon: Toward a Theory of Revisionism* (1982), *The American Religion* (1992), *The Western Canon* (1994), and *Omens of Millennium: The Gnosis of Angels, Dreams, and Resurrection* (1996). *The Anxiety of Influence* (1973) sets forth Professor Bloom's provocative theory of the literary relationships between the great writers and their predecessors. His most recent books include *Shakespeare: The Invention of the Human* (1998), a 1998 National Book Award finalist, *How to Read and Why* (2000), *Genius: A Mosaic of One Hundred Exemplary Creative Minds* (2002), and *Hamlet: Poem Unlimited* (2003). In 1999, Professor Bloom received the prestigious American Academy of Arts and Letters Gold Medal for Criticism, and in 2002 he received the Catalonia International Prize.

Alan Cheuse is a Professor at the George Mason University Graduate Creative Writing Program. He is the author, among other works of fiction, of the novels *The Light Possessed* (1990) and *The Grandmothers' Club* (1988), and the recent story collection *Lost and Old River* (1998). His articles, magazine journalism, and reviews have also appeared widely. Cheuse also serves as book commentator for National Public Radio's "All Things Considered."

Vereen M. Bell is Professor of English at Vanderbilt University, where he has been a member of the faculty since 1961. Areas of expertise include modern British and American literature, film study and modern critical theory. His book *The Achievement of Cormac McCarthy* (1988) was the first published book-length work on McCarthy.

Nell Sullivan earned a Ph.D. in English from Rice University and is currently Associate Professor of English at the University of Houston-Downtown, where she teaches American literature. Her essays have appeared in *African American Review*, *Southern Quarterly*, and *Mississippi Quarterly*, and she is currently working on a book-length study of gender in McCarthy's fiction.

Phillip A. Snyder is the American Studies Coordinator and Associate Professor of English at Brigham Young University. He specializes in twentieth-century British and American literature, studies in autobiography, and American regional and ethnic literature. He is active in several academic societies and is co-director of the Society for Studies in American Autobiography, as well as a board member of the Utah Western Heritage Foundation.

Tom Pilkington taught at Southwest Texas State University and Texas Christian University before joining Tarleton State University's Department of English and Languages in 1969. Dr. Pilkington is author or editor of thirteen books, including *My Blood's Country: Studies in Southwestern Literature* (1973), *Critical Essays on the Western American Novel* (1981), *Careless Weeds: Six Texas Novellas* (1993), and, most recently, *State of Mind: Texas Literature and Culture* (1998). He has published many articles as well, in both scholarly journals and popular magazines, and is a regular book reviewer for the *Dallas Morning News* and the *Houston Chronicle* newspapers.

Edwin T. Arnold is a Professor of English at Appalachian State University in Boone, North Carolina. He has published widely on William Faulkner, Donald Harington, Erskine Caldwell, and Cormac McCarthy. He is co-editor with Dianne Luce of *Perspectives on Cormac McCarthy* (1999) and *A Cormac McCarthy Companion: The Border Trilogy* (2001).

Mark Busby is Director of the Center for the Study of the Southwest and Professor of English at Southwest Texas State University. He has published widely, including articles and stories. His books include *Larry McMurtry and the West: An Ambivalent Relationship* (1995) and *Ralph Ellison* (1991). He is coeditor (with Dick Heaberlin) of *Southwestern American Literature*, and since fall 1996, *Texas Books in Review*.

Sara L. Spurgeon is completing a Ph.D. in western American literature at the University of Arizona in Tucson. She is the co-author, with Dr. David K. Dunaway, of the 1995 nonfiction study *Writing the Southwest*.

Nancy Kreml is the Humanities and ESL Department Chair at Midlands Technical College, in Columbia, SC, where she has taught for about twenty-five years. She received a Ph.D. in Linguistics from the University of South Carolina in 1992.

Dianne C. Luce chairs the English Department at Midlands Technical College in Columbia, South Carolina. She has published several articles on Cormac McCarthy, and published books on William Faulkner. She is co-editor with Edwin T. Arnold of *Perspectives on Cormac McCarthy* (1999) and *A Cormac McCarthy Companion: The Border Trilogy* (2001).

John Wegner is an Assistant Professor at Angelo State University. He received his Ph.D. at the University of North Texas in 1997. He has published several articles on McCarthy, and was editor of *The Cormac McCarthy Journal Online*.

Acknowledgments

"A Note on Landscape in *All The Pretty Horses*" by Alan Cheuse. From *The Southern Quarterly* 30, (Summer 1992): pp. 140–42. © 1992 by *The Southern Quarterly*. Reprinted by permission of *The Southern Quarterly*.

"Between the Wish and the Thing the World Lies Waiting" by Vereen M. Bell. From *The Southern Review* 28, no. 4 (October 1992): pp. 924–25. Copyright © 1992. Reprinted by permission of the author.

"Boys Will Be Boys And Girls Will Be Gone" by Nell Sullivan. From *A Cormac McCarthy Companion: The Border Trilogy*. Ed. Edwin T. Arnold and Dianne C. Luce. Jackson: University Press of Mississippi, 2001: pp. 228–255. © 2001 by University Press of Mississippi. Originally printed in *The Southern Quarterly* 38, no. 3 (Spring 2000), pp. 167–185. Reprinted by permission of *The Southern Quarterly*.

"Cowboy Codes in Cormac McCarthy's Border Trilogy" by Phillip A. Snyder. From *A Cormac McCarthy Companion: The Border Trilogy*. Ed. Edwin T. Arnold and Dianne C. Luce. Jackson: University Press of Mississippi, 2001: pp. 198, 200–203. © 2001 by University Press of Mississippi. Originally printed in *The Southern Quarterly* 38, no. 3 (Spring 2000), pp. 147–166. Reprinted by permission of *The Southern Quarterly*.

"Fate and Free Will on the American Frontier: Cormac McCarthy's Western Fiction" by Tom Pilkington. From *Western American Literature* 27 (Winter 1993): pp. 318–22. This article originally appeared in the September 1992 issue of *The World & I* and is reprinted by permission of *The World & I*, a publication of the Washington Times Corporation. Copyright © 1992.

"'Go to Sleep': Dreams and Visions in the Border Trilogy" by Edwin T. Arnold. From *A Cormac McCarthy Companion: The Border Trilogy*. Ed. Edwin T. Arnold and Dianne C. Luce. Jackson: University Press of Mississippi, 2001: pp. 49–57. © 2001 by University Press of Mississippi. Originally printed in *The Southern Quarterly* 38, no. 3 (Spring 2000), pp. 34–58. Reprinted by permission of *The Southern Quarterly*.

"Into the Darkening Land, the World to Come: Cormac McCarthy's Border Crossings" by Mark Busby. From *Myth, Legend, Dust: Critical Responses to Cormac McCarthy*. Ed. Rick Wallach. New York: Manchester University Press, 2000: pp. 227–248. © 2000 by Manchester University Press. Reprinted by permission of Manchester University Press.

"'Pledged in Blood': Truth and Redemption in Cormac McCarthy's *All The Pretty Horses*" by Sara L. Spurgeon. From *Western American Literature* 34 (1) (Spring 1999): pp. 25, 27–30, 34–35, 40. Copyright © 1999. Reprinted by permission of Utah State University.

"Stylistic Variation and Cognitive Constraint in *All The Pretty Horses*" by Nancy Kreml. From *Sacred Violence: A Reader's Companion to Cormac McCarthy*. Ed. Wade Hall and Rick Wallach. El Paso: Texas Western Press, 1995: pp. 137–48. © 1995 by Texas Western Press. Reprinted by permission of Texas Western Press.

"'When You Wake': John Grady Cole's Heroism in *All The Pretty Horses*," by Dianne C. Luce. From *Sacred Violence: A Reader's Companion to Cormac McCarthy*. Ed. Wade Hall and Rick Wallach. El Paso: Texas Western Press, 1995: pp. 155–164. © 1995 by Texas Western Press. Reprinted by permission of Texas Western Press.

"Whose Story is It? History and Fiction in Cormac McCarthy's *All The Pretty Horses*" by John Wegner. From *The Southern Quarterly* 36, no. 2 (Winter 1998): pp. 103–108. © 1998 by *The Southern Quarterly*. Reprinted by permission of *The Southern Quarterly*.

Index

and last action hero, 97
as leader, 22, 65
and leaving La Vega, 46–47
his limitation of self, 84
his loss, 17
and lost dreams, 44
and love of horses, 74
his loyalty, 27, 34
and manhood, 49
his mentor, 45–46
his mother, 64
and moving back in history, 61
his parents divorce, 18
his personal desires, 79
and prison fight, 40
and protagonist, 13
his psychological journey, 49
his reality, 34, 38
his redemption, 90–91
and regaining paradise, 97
his responsibility, 50–51
his return to La Purisima, 42–44
his return to Texas, 51
and revenging his past, 48
and sale of ranch, 17–18
and similarities to *Hamlet*, 77
and the storm, 57
his troubles, 99
and understanding himself, 40
his venture to Mexico, 99
and the vision, 77
and wanting the past, 21

H

Hacienda de Nuestra Senora de la Purisima Concepcion, 28–29, 33, 35, 78
and Grady's return to, 42–43, 80
Hamlet, (Shakespeare), 7–8, 77
Hanrahan, Gene Z., 104
Hector, Don, character in *All the Pretty Horses*, 30–31, 34, 36, 44, 78, 101, 104–105
his opinion of Grady, 98

his ranch, 78
and the truth about Grady, 98
Hemingway, Ernest, 37, 75
Holleman, Lee, 9
Huckleberry Finn, (Twain), 59, 84

I

Ingram-Merrill Award, 9

J

Jarrett, Robert
and comparison of Grady and Alfonsa, 45
and heterosexual romance, 63

K

Knight, Alan, 104
Knopf, Alfred A.
and McCarthy's publisher, 13
Kreml, Nancy, 38, 92–96
and transparent style, 37

L

LaFrontera
and north/south border, 83
Landscape, 56–58
Landscape and the Novel in Mexico, (essay), Paz, 56
Lilley, James D., 21
Luce, Dianne C., 18, 20, 23, 40, 53, 97–103

M

Mac Arthur Fellowship, 10, 12
Macbeth, (Shakespeare), 7
Madero, 104, 107
his affect on Mexico, 106
his cultural influence, 105
McCarthy, Cormac, 7
and action, 73, 76
his birth, 9
and border crossings, 83–85
his characters, 60–61, 63
and compared to Faulkner, 11
and the cowboy code, 68–69